Questions and Answers that tell
hundreds of fascinating facts
about our planet

WHERE IN THE WORLD?

by Philip S. Egan

FOREWORD BY JANE McGUIGAN

Illustrations by David Cunningham and Rand McNally

RAND McNALLY & COMPANY

Chicago • New York • San Francisco

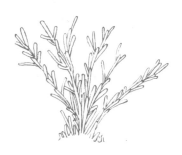

TO OUR READERS

Once upon a time Robert Louis Stevenson, an English poet, wrote a poem which begins,

The world is so full of a number of things. . . .

And of course it is—wonderfully interesting things!

As we think about our world, we have questions. How old is it? Where did all the water come from that fills the lakes and rivers and oceans? Why don't we fly off of the earth as it spins? Why do earthquakes happen? What makes a volcano erupt? What makes the wind blow? And why is the wind sometimes a gentle breeze, sometimes a violent storm? There are so many questions!

We learn by asking questions. When you have questions such as these about our world, whom can you ask for answers? Sometimes your parents, or your older brothers and sisters, can help you. Sometimes your teachers can. Sometimes none of them can answer you. What do you do then? You ask a specialist.

This book has been made for you by such specialists. They have chosen questions most frequently asked about our world, and have answered them for you. You may read it through, from beginning to end, or you may open it anywhere and browse. Either way, you will find a store of surprising and fascinating information about our world.

If you have a globe or an atlas which you can use as you read this book, you will find that you learn still more. Even without these helps, though, the book will give you a wealth of interesting knowledge about the where, how, and why of things you see about you every day, things you hear about on news broadcasts, places you read about.

What questions do *you* have about the world?

JANE McGUIGAN

CONTENTS

WHERE
IN THE
WORLD

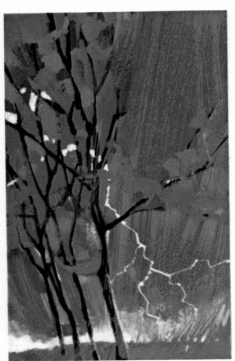  

RAIN   ICE   PLANT GROWTH

How old is the world?

Current scientific estimates place the age of the earth at about five billion years. Throughout the course of modern scientific investigation, this estimate has undergone constant change. Only twenty or thirty years ago figures of two billion years were commonly used in scientific circles. Unless we have finally arrived at the possession of enough knowledge to estimate the age of the earth conclusively, the figure will continue to change as additional information and new findings become available.

There are a number of theories about the earth's formation that experts consider have valid points. But many details remain to be cleared up before we can even be sure if the earth started out as a cold, inert body and then heated up, or if it started as a molten body and is now cooling down.

One of the important reasons for man's wish to venture into space is to find out more about the earth. If we can get to the moon and find out how old that sphere is, we may be able to relate that knowledge to

WIND

SNOW

EROSION

Through the ages the earth has been shaped by the influences of weather.

the earth's beginnings. The moon is so removed from the changes that have occurred on earth that it may be possible to go back countless ages in the study. Earth has an atmosphere and all of the influences that go with it—rain, erosion, plant growth, vast seas, wind, snow and ice. The moon is perhaps entirely free of these effects and may show us a picture almost unchanged by time.

How big is the world?

It is 7,926 miles in diameter at the equator, and 7,900 miles in diameter through the poles. The variation in the figures shows that the earth is not truly round, that it has a slight pear shape which is due to the spinning of the globe. As it spins, the speed at the equator is about 1,000 miles per hour. This is enough speed to pull the ball out of shape at this mid-belt and make it a little fatter there.

One way to prove the world is round.

Where in the world
can you see the curvature of the earth?

Although with a quick glance you can't notice any curvature of the earth, observation at certain locations will show it.

From the shore of a large lake, or the ocean, you can see about fourteen miles over the water. Yet the approach of a ship that is farther away than fourteen miles can be detected. At first smoke from the ship's funnels will seem to be coming up out of the water. As the ship draws closer to shore, the masts will come into view and the funnels will appear. Then the captain's bridge, the cabins, and finally the hull itself will be seen. Only one thing can explain this behavior: the surface of the water must be curved. If the surface were flat, the entire ship would be seen as soon as it came close enough to be visible.

Another proof of the earth's curving surface is available in today's jet age. The trail of a jet aircraft, flying high and at a constant height and direction, will appear curved when you look up at it from the ground. The trail sweeping across the sky for a great distance in reality is a streak that is parallel to the surface of the earth.

One of the best proofs of the curvature of earth is found at the time of an eclipse of the moon. As the shadow of the earth from the sun's light goes across the face of the moon, the shadow is clearly that of a circular body. There, before your eyes, 238,862 miles away, is the round shadow of the earth creeping across the moon's surface.

Where in the world do earthquakes occur?

In Japan, and such other places as California, Alaska, China, and Turkey, severe earth shocks are felt quite often, and damage is done at times. But there are other parts of the world that seem very quiet, and where not even the dishes have ever rattled from a tremor. The sensitive instruments that scientists use to record earthquakes show, however, that tremors happen just about everywhere and can be recorded all over the world. Only the more intense shocks make the newspapers or television news programs.

Are all mountains about the same age?

Not any more than people or plants or animals. Unlike people, though, the more wrinkled a mountain, the younger it probably is. Rugged, sharp mountains such as the American Rockies or the Swiss Alps are quite "young," perhaps sixty million years old. The Cascade Range on the west coast of the United States may be only one million years old, born yesterday in geological terms. On the other hand, such ranges as the Appalachians along the east coast of the United States have been rounded and worn smooth by countless rains, snows, and frosts, with constant erosion by the winds, and they may be as much as two hundred million years old. Some mountains, for example, the Laurentians in Canada, are so old that they have almost disappeared.

Arctic Ocean

FRANZ JOSEF LAND (SOV. UN.)

NOVAYA ZEMLYA
C. ZHELANIYA

SEVERNAYA ZEMLYA

C. CHELYUSKIN

NEW SIBERIAN ISLANDS
KOTELNY FADDEYEV

NOVAYA SIBIR

East Siberian Sea

WRANGEL I.

PT. BARROW

Beaufort Sea

C. BATHURST

PRINCE OF WALES
LANDS E

Kara Sea

Laptev Sea

75°

TAYMYR PENINSULA

Arctic Circle

Nordvik

Tiksi

Allaykha

Verkhoyansk

Kolyma

Ambarchik

ANADYR RANGE

Bering Str.

BROOKS RA.

Nome

ALASKA

Dawson

MT. McKINLEY 20,320 FT.

Sim

Mackenzie

Vorkuta

Dudinka

Igarka

Salekhard

Yeniseysk

Arctic Circle

Nizhnyaya Tunguska

Olekminsk

YERKHOYANSK MTS.

Yakutsk

Seymchan

GYDAN MTS.

Anadyr

ST. LAWRENCE

Yukon

Fairbanks

Anchorage

60°

SOVIET UNION

Tomsk

Krasnoyarsk

Kirensk

Aldan

DZHUGDZHUR

Okhotsk

KAMCHATKA PEN.

ST. MATTHEW I.

Gulf of Alaska

Sitka

Juneau

Sverdlovsk

Omsk

Novosibirsk

NUNIVAK I.

ALASKA PEN.

KODIAK I.

ALEXANDER ARCH.

Ketchikan

Chelyabinsk

Barnaul

Novokuznetsk

Nikolayevsk

KOMANDORSKIYE IS.

PRIBILOF IS.

Bering Sea

QUEEN CHARLOTTE IS.

Van

Karaganda

Semipalatinsk

SAYAN MTS.

Komsomolsk

Sea of Okhotsk

Petropavlovsk

ATTU Dutch Harbor

VANCOUVER

Se

Balkhash

Kyzyl

Khabarovsk

SAKHALIN

C. LOPATKA

KISKA

ALEUTIAN IS.

Po

45°

L. Balkhash

Ulan Bator

MONGOLIA

GOBI DESERT

A S I A

MANCHURIA

Vladivostok

KURILS (SOV. UN.)

Hakodate

North

San Fran

Aral Sea

Alma-Ata

Tashkent

Samarkand

Urumchi

Yarkand

Peking

Mukden

Sea of Japan

HOKKAIDŌ

Kabul

AFGHANISTAN

Rawalpindi

PAK.

KUNLUN MTS.

Lanchow

Tientsin

Tsingtao

KOREA

Pyongyang

Seoul

Kyoto

HONSHŪ

Tōkyō

JAPAN

Nagoya

MIDWAY IS.

HAWAIIAN ISLANDS (U.S.A.)

30°

IRAN

Lahore

Delhi

MT. EVEREST 29,028

HIMALAYA MTS.

NEPAL BHU.

CHINA

Chengtu

Chungking

Changsha

Nanking

Wuhan

Shanghai

Kitakyūshū

Osaka

Tropic of Cancer

BONIN IS.

OAHU

Honolulu

HAWAII

New Delhi

Hyderabad

Ganges

Kunming

Foochow

TAIWAN (FORMOSA)

GUA

Karachi

INDIA

Calcutta

Dacca

Hanoi

Canton

HAINAN

LUZON

Philippine Sea

WAKE (U.S.A.)

Bombay

Arabian Sea

Hyderabad

Bay of Bengal

Rangoon

BURMA

South China

Manila

Quezon City

MARIANA ISLANDS (U.S.A. TRUST)

BIKINI I.

MARSHALL

15°

Bangalore

Madras

Kozhikode

ANDAMAN IS. (INDIA)

THAILAND

Bangkok

CAMB.

Saigon

VIET NAM

PHILIPPINES

MINDANAO

GUAM (U.S.A.)

CAROLINE

PONAPE ISLANDS (U.S.A. TRUST)

Colombo

CEYLON

NICOBAR IS. (INDIA)

G. of Siam

MALAYSIA

PALMYRA (BR. & U.S.A.)

MALDIVE ISLANDS

DONDRA HEAD

Singapore

BORNEO

CELEBES

EAST INDIES

HALMAHERA

ISLANDS (U.S.A. TRUST)

TARAWA

GILBERT ISLANDS

CHRISTMAS (BR. & U.S.A.)

Equa

0°

CHAGOS IS. (BR.)

Equator

Padang

SUMATRA

INDONESIA

Djakarta

JAVA

Java Sea

Banda Sea

CELEBES

WEST IRIAN (INDON. ADMIN.)

NEW GUINEA (AUSTL. ADMIN. & UNION TRUST)

BISMARCK ARCH. (AUSTL.)

NAURU (AUSTL. BR. & N.Z. TRUST)

JARVIS (U.S.A.)

STARBUCK (BR. & U.S.A.)

MALDEN (BR. & U.S.A.)

MARQUESAS I. (FR.)

Indian

COCOS IS. (KEELING) (AUSTL.)

CHRISTMAS (AUSTL.)

SUMBA

Arafura Sea

NEW BRITAIN

SOLOMON ISLANDS (BR.)

ELLICE IS. (BR.)

TOKELAU (N.Z.)

TONGAREVA (N.Z.)

MANIHIKI IS. (N.Z.)

TUAMOTU

Ocean

Equator

Timor Sea

Darwin

PAPUA

Port Moresby

GREAT

Coral Sea

WESTERN SAMOA

Apia

SOCIETY IS. (FR.)

TAHITI

Papeete

LOW ARCHIPELA. (FR.)

15°

Tropic of Capricorn

NORTH WEST CAPE

Broome

Cairns

Townsville

GREAT BARRIER REEF

NEW HEBRIDES (BR. & FR.)

FIJI IS.

Suva

NEW CALEDONIA (FR.)

LOYALTY IS. (FR.)

TONGA IS. (BR.)

COOK IS. (N.Z.)

Tropic of Capricorn

PITCAIRN (BR.)

South P a

Carnarvon

Geraldton

AUSTRALIA

Alice Springs

GREAT VICTORIA DESERT

Brisbane

30°

Ocean

Fremantle

C. LEEUWIN

Perth

Albany

Great Australian Bight

Adelaide

Darling

Newcastle

Sydney

Canberra

Melbourne

KERMADEC IS. (N.Z.)

NORTH ISLAND

Auckland

Gisborne

NEW ZEALAND

SOUTH ISLAND

Wellington

Oc

AMSTERDAM (FR.)

ST. PAUL (FR.)

Bass Strait

TASMANIA

Hobart

Tasman Sea

Invercargill

Dunedin

Christchurch

CHATHAM IS. (N.Z.)

45°

KERGUELEN (FR.)

AUCKLAND IS. (N.Z.)

ANTIPODES (N.Z.)

BOUNTY IS. (N.Z.)

HEARD (AUSTL.)

CAMPBELL (N.Z.)

MC DONALD (AUSTL.)

MACQUARIE (AUSTL.)

60°

SHACKLETON ICE SHELF

WEST ICE SHELF

C. GOODENOUGH

BALLENY IS.

A

Antarctic Circle

C. DARNLEY

C. PENCK

C. HOADLEY

WILKES LAND

C. WILLIAMS

C. ADARE

75°

MAC-ROBERTSON COAST

AMERY ICE SHELF

AMERICAN HIGHLAND

VICTORIA LAND

Ross Sea

ROSS I.

Little America

MT. EREBUS 12,280 FT.

ROOSEVELT I.

C. WILSON

ROSS ICE SHELF

Wrigl

MARI

MT. MARKHAM 14,272 FT.

A N T A R C T I C A

A-510000-22- -5
COSMO SERIES WORLD
RAND McNALLY & COMPANY
Made in U. S. A.

Longitude East of Greenwich

Longitude West of Greenwich

75° 90° 105° 120° 135° 150° 165° 180° 165° 150° 135°

20

The world portrayed as a map, on a Miller cylindrical projection. (See page 58.)

How can there be deserts near large bodies of water?

The fact that there is a great amount of water nearby doesn't always mean that the land will be well watered and thick with vegetation. Winds that blow off the water may not go in the right direction. Or the air coming off the water may be dried out by the heat of the land, or held back by some obstacle. In the case of the great Sahara Desert in Africa, the Atlas Mountains keep the moist air of the Mediterranean Sea from reaching that vast area, and to a great extent the air in that part of the world is dense and dry anyhow.

Deserts generally occur in a belt above and below the equator, where the prevailing winds have lost their moisture to lands north or south. Further, it must be recognized that moisture in the air is not enough to bring rain. Air must be cooled to have the moisture in it "wrung out." This can come about if the air meets a cool land mass, or another mass of cooler air, or if the air is caused to rise to high altitude by a rising slope of land or an abrupt mountain range. Air can be "soaking wet" and drift past parched land.

The Atlas Mountains hem in the coast of North Africa.

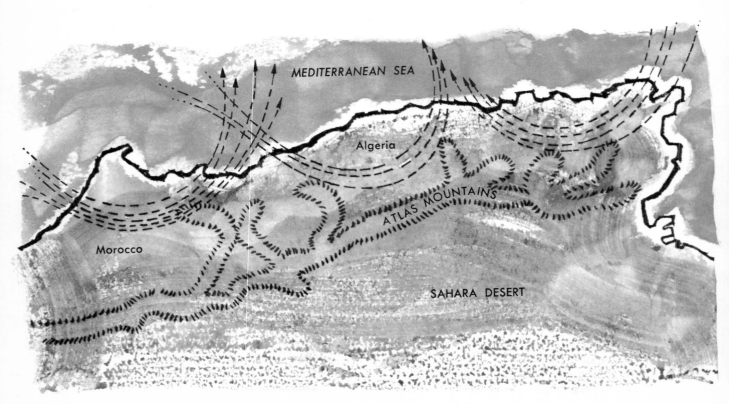

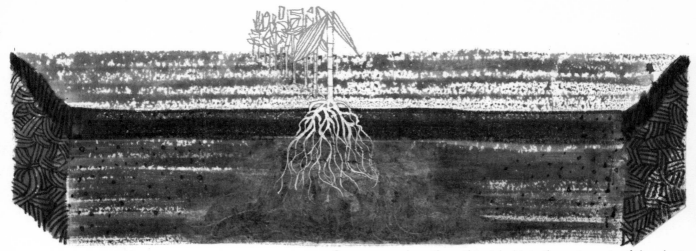

Corn grows where the soil is rich. Note the main roots of the plant are in the topsoil, but some do extend down into the subsoil.

How deep is the soil?

Even at its deepest, it is like a sprinkling of dust on the surface of the earth. But, in man's terms and eyes, that dust is a matter of life or death, of food or no food. Soil is a precious resource. The southwest region of the North American continent has vast areas where the soil is very poor and only a few inches deep. Exposed rock, mountains, buttes, and boulders cover much of the area. Even where it is a thick, rich topsoil, as in the cornbelt of Iowa, the soil may be only a few feet deep. The deepest soil goes many feet down, still a paltry depth compared to the 3,959-mile distance to the center of the earth.

Is all soil equally good for growing crops?

The fact that there is a lot of soil doesn't always mean that it is good soil for many crops, however. One of the big problems in increasing the areas used to grow food crops in the world is that appearances are deceiving. The lush forests of the well-watered equatorial lands of Africa and South America are not so rich, after all, when cleared and planted. The excessive heat of the region causes bacteria to thrive in the soil, and these then keep the soil from being suited to a variety of crops. Man has found that the task of converting land is not a simple one.

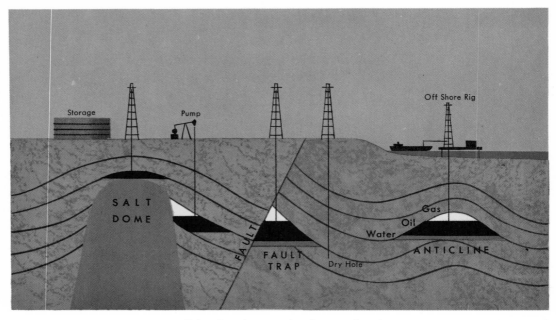

Oil is found trapped in layers of rock, sometimes in an upthrust rock layer along a fault, or in an anticline, a sedimentary dome formation.

How did oil get into the ground?

Scientists aren't certain just how oil was made by nature, but they know that it was formed millions of years ago when the remains of primitive forms of life settled at the bottom of the seas. Large collections of these organisms turned into drops of oil, and as the floor of the sea was covered with sediment, the oil became trapped in pools. The sediment took many shapes and formed different kinds of rock over the countless years. During this time the surface of the earth was subjected to buckling, uplifting, lowering, and sliding.

The sea bottom of prehistoric times may be thousands of feet above sea level today, due to uplifting. Or the ancient sea bottom may lie deep under today's dry land or ocean, due to lowering. It is the pools of oil trapped under rock, formed in prehistoric times, that man taps today for his huge oil supply needs. Every time the family car starts up and moves off on some errand, it is running on a part of the remains of billions upon billions of primitive organisms that lived millions of years ago!

Do you have a map address?

Your street address is a number along a known and real path, the street or road or route where your home is found. This arrangement is perfectly satisfactory if a person on foot or in a car wants to find you. Even a stranger can get directions from the local gas station or drug store and easily make his way. But for travel over long distances on land that has no roads, or on the open sea, man has had to devise a system that allows him to give any place its own special number.

To and from the North and South Poles men have agreed upon the use of *lines of longitude,* or *meridians.* These are laid out so that they divide the surface of the earth into degrees east or west of a starting line that runs through Greenwich, England. This starting line is commonly referred to as the *Prime Meridian.* It gives man a way to say where he is as far as east or west is concerned.

To get a way of locating places north or south, man then divided the earth's surface into *lines of latitude,* or *parallels,* which are *degrees* north or south of the *equator.* The equator is the mid-belt of the earth, running all the way around, halfway between the North and South Poles.

By using numbers, you can determine the address of any place on earth. For example, Greenwich is 0 degrees longitude, of course, but it is 51¼ degrees north of the equator. Therefore, its map address is "0° long., 51¼° N. lat."; New Orleans' is "90° W. long., 30° N. lat." By using a map or a globe you can figure out your map address.

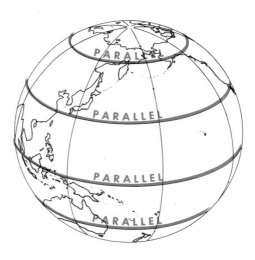

All meridians are the same length and they come together at the poles. Parallels are the same distance apart, but they get shorter in circumference as they approach the poles.

Why do we have lightning and thunder?

In the turbulent center of towering storm clouds, rising air cools and the moisture it contains condenses into raindrops. These drops are constantly breaking apart and rejoining, building an electrical charge as they do so. When the charge becomes great enough, electrical energy is released. We see this release of electrical energy as a bolt of lightning. It may occur high in the cloud top, between two clouds, or between a cloud and the ground.

The lightning bolt, tremendously powerful, sets up a shock wave in the air which we hear as thunder. You can tell how far away a storm is by listening. The farther away from the observer the lightning bolt is, the greater will be the length of time between his seeing the lightning and his hearing the thunder. Sound travels at about 750 miles per hour at sea level. This is about one-fifth of a mile per second. A thunder clap heard five seconds after seeing lightning will mean, therefore, that the lightning was about a mile away. Some summer day, try measuring the distance away of an oncoming electrical storm. By using a watch with a second hand, you can determine the number of seconds that elapse between the lightning and the thunder. Then divide this number by five to get the number of miles.

Is there any difference between weather and climate?

There's a good deal of difference. Comparing weather and climate is rather like comparing a person's mood with his general disposition. Youngsters might say, for instance, "My teacher, Mrs. Brown, was in a very bad mood this morning (the weather), but she's really a nice person most of the time (the climate)."

It's not uncommon for some areas to have temperature, rain or snowfall, and wind extremes over short periods of time that lead to the old saying that "if you don't like the *weather,* wait twenty minutes." In Chicago, for instance, a record heat wave in the spring may be followed in two days by record cold for that date. Weather fronts will frequently perform a tug-of-war, backed by masses of heated or chilled air from the south or north. As a front passes a particular spot, it may expose an area to extremes of weather that are far from normal. Snow has been known to fall in Los Angeles, California and Fort Myers, Florida. Electrical storms have occurred in midwinter in the northern United States. But *climate* is the average of all weather conditions over the entire year, year after year. Based on this long-time average, a given area can be expected to have a general pattern that places it in a certain climate category—tropical, temperate, arctic, etc.

What did "54-40 or fight" mean?

By the convention of 1818, the Canada-United States boundary was fixed along a line of latitude 49 degrees north, from the Lake of the Woods to the Rockies. At the time both nations claimed the Pacific Coast area, then known as the Oregon Territory, which stretched from Spanish California to Alaska, and both nations occupied it.

American immigrants settled in Oregon over the years, a provisional government was formed, and United States politics entered the picture. The campaign that resulted in James K. Polk's election to the presidency stirred up a demand for the British to get out of Oregon entirely, and for the border to be fixed at *54 degrees 40 minutes North*—"54-40 or fight."

As president, Polk grew more reasonable, and in 1846 a compromise was made with the British that extended the 49th parallel as the Canada-United States border all the way to the Pacific. There was no fight.

A twisting funnel cloud warns of an approaching tornado.

What causes hurricanes and tornadoes?

In an area of calm over a warm tropical sea, the sun will heat the moist air and cause it to rise in a huge column. Air nearby will slowly start a general flow toward this heated "chimney." As the process gains force, the air will turn as it nears the center and form a spiral, a twist. Many days of this air movement under a tropical sun can bring on tremendous wind speeds and a *hurricane* many miles across will start. A hurricane, therefore, is a large storm, over a great area, which is born at sea. If the whole storm wanders to land areas, awesome destruction can be brought to places where people live.

A *tornado* is a small local storm of fierce wind speeds that comes from a larger, but not nearly as fierce, storm condition. At times a combination of "fronts" of warm moist air and cold dry air will cross each other at an angle that will start columns of air twisting at high speed. Given the right "push" long enough, one of these funnels of air, the black twister of a tornado, will extend from the clouds of the storm front and reach the ground. Wind speeds of as much as 500 miles per hour are believed to exist in some tornado funnels.

A tornado, then, is a concentrated, brief, local storm. It has fabulous power in a small area. As the larger parent storm moves, the funnel of

Winds of hurricanes exceed seventy-three miles per hour.

the tornado may move in a path along the ground, also. It is possible to watch a tornado tear houses to shreds while you are only hundreds of feet away. It is not likely that you could safely watch a hurricane tear a sea wall apart from a short distance away.

Why is the water level so high in a hurricane?

A hurricane is a storm noted for a low barometer. The instrument used to measure the pressure of the atmosphere, that is the weight of the air above any given point, always shows a low reading during hurricane conditions. And during the storm the seas will rise along the ravaged shore because the reduced air pressure that accompanies the storm has allowed the water level to rise in a gigantic mound, many miles in diameter. This condition results in raging winds and onrushing waves. Away from the hurricane, more normal air pressures will prevail and push the sea level down to its usual state.

A hurricane is the unhappy combination of weather conditions that can flood a coast. In the 1938 hurricane in New England, water levels of over eighteen feet above normal were reported at Fall River.

Does a compass always point to the North Pole?

Hardly ever, oddly enough. The compass is a strip or bar of magnetized metal that takes advantage of the facts that the earth is magnetic and that a magnet will tend to point along a north-south direction. With the metal bar of the compass set over a card that indicates various directions, or with a card fastened to the strip itself and the assembly allowed to pivot freely, the instrument is almost magic in behavior. But it has its faults. The compass will point close enough to the true direction of the North Pole to be of real use, but you must know how much it is in error to use it correctly.

Compasses always point to the *magnetic pole,* which is not at the true pole, and changes its location over the years. Today the magnetic pole is near Prince of Wales Island, north of the Canadian mainland; following the turn of the century it was on Boothia Peninsula, three hundred miles away. Also, because of slight differences in the magnetism of our earth in various locations, there will be a variation that will influence the compass' reading. If these are known, the compass is an extremely useful tool of navigation.

Is the air really "empty"?

The air—our atmosphere—may be clear enough to call transparent, but it is by no means empty. It is a mixture of gases that humans absolutely must breathe to live. It is also a mixture of gases strong enough to blow a house down (a windstorm), float a one-hundred-and-fifty-ton object (a jet airliner moving fast enough), carry tons of water and ice (rain and snow), and act as a shield (by keeping harmful rays in the sun's light from scorching us). Air is so heavy that, at sea level, it pushes in on us with nearly fifteen pounds of pressure for every square inch of our bodies, a tremendous weight we never even feel.

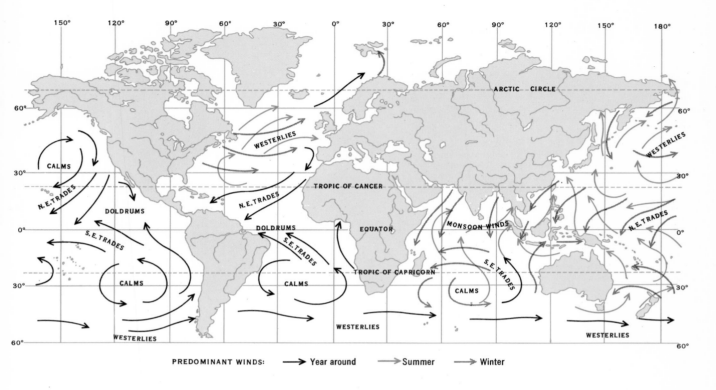

The atmosphere surrounding the earth is always in motion. Winds over the world have various prevailing directions, but are influenced by areas of land and sea and by the seasons.

Why does the wind blow?

The air that envelops the surface of the earth is not uniformly dense. It is heaviest at the surface, thinning out as it extends upward, practically vanishing at one hundred miles altitude. This air is heated and chilled to different degrees all over the world. As it is heated it rises and thins, and heavier or cooler air next to it moves in to replace it. At the same time, this air is floating around the huge ball that is our earth, which is spinning at 1,000 miles per hour in some places. The spin also causes the air to move. On a large scale, over land and sea, the movement of air will be anything from a gentle breeze to a gale.

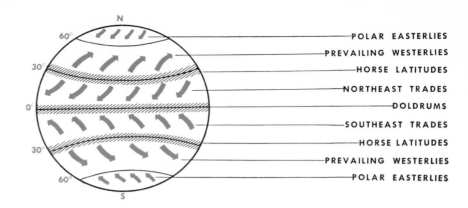

A basic diagram of the prevailing pattern of wind direction north and south of the equator.

What are doldrums?

In the equatorial latitudes of the earth, the canopy of air that surrounds our planet is constantly heated by the direct rays of the sun. The heated air rises to higher altitudes and flows northward and southward. Near the earth's surface, the rising air is replaced by cooler masses of air moving in from the north and south, meeting at the equatorial belt. In the northern summer, the latitude where the air masses meet is somewhat north of the actual equator; during the southern summer, this latitude is somewhat south of the actual equator. The latitudes where the air masses come together is the area of the doldrums. As these immense masses of air from the north and south approach each other, they slow down. They drift slowly westward and upward. For sailing ships this climatic feature was a source of concern. While by no means the only latitude where calms would be experienced, the doldrums made crossing the equator a hot and dreary experience. The doldrums still can be a vexing problem to men waiting in a schooner or on a life raft for a steady wind to fill the sails.

Do trade winds always blow in one direction?

Always is a word meaning perpetually and invariably, and it comes quite close to describing the trade winds. The horse latitudes lie at 30 degrees north and 30 degrees south of the doldrums, a region of equatorial variables and calms. The trade winds are generated here. Given a twist by the rotation of the earth (the Coriolis force), the air masses move from the northeast above the equator, and the southeast below it, into a beltlike region between the equatorial doldrums and the horse latitudes.

Christopher Columbus, the master mariner, was the first man to take advantage of the great trade winds. In his African voyages, Columbus had observed the steady *easterly* trade winds between the equator and the latitude of the Canary Islands. In formulating his plan to sail west to the East Indies, he decided to sail south from Spain to the Canaries and to start west from these islands, taking advantage of the steady east winds.

Columbus' plan let him succeed in finding land even though it was not the Indies that he wanted. All previous attempts in sailing west had met with failure because the ships had set out from Portugal toward the Azores. To sail west from the Azores, one has to buck *westerly* winds. Columbus was the first of many sailors to recognize the constancy of the brisk trade winds, and to take advantage of their almost mechanical regularity.

What is the highest
wind velocity ever recorded?

Wind speeds of 500 miles per hour may exist in the funnel of a tornado, although no measurement of this speed by instruments has ever been made. We must rely on records of special mountain weather stations for official figures of wind speeds. The station on Mount Washington, New Hampshire, at an altitude of 6,248 feet, has recorded winds of as much as 231 miles per hour. This station is also the location of the highest annual average winds, recorded at 36.9 miles per hour.

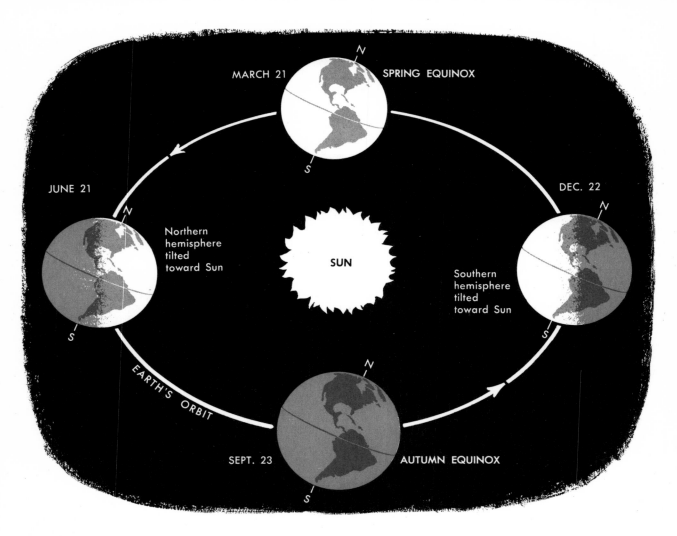

Why do we have seasons?

The earth moves, or revolves, around a star which we call the sun. As it revolves, it rotates, or spins, so that any point on the surface of the earth is in sunlight part of the time and in shadow the rest of the time. This makes day and night. During the time it takes to travel around the sun, the earth makes 365¼ complete rotations, a period of time we call a year.

As it goes around the sun, the earth's day-and-night spinning is on an axis which is along an imaginary line running from the North Pole to the South Pole. This axis of the earth is tilted at an angle of 23½ degrees in its path around the sun. In June the tilt brings northern lands into a more direct line with the sun's rays and allows more of their heat to reach the northern part of the world than the southern. Then there is summer in the United States and Canada and the other lands in the Northern Hemisphere. At the same time, countries like Argentina and Australia in the Southern Hemisphere are having winter.

Six months later, as the earth has traveled half its distance around the sun, the southern part of the world will be receiving the more direct rays of the sun and more heat will get to it. Then Argentina and Australia and other southern lands will have their summer, and winter will have moved into the northern lands. Between these times, the heat will steadily change from one extreme to the other, progressing from a warmer to colder season back to a warmer season.

The annual path of the earth about the sun gives us seasons. The equinoxes (equal day and night length) occur in the spring and fall. The tilt of the earth's axis causes the Northern Hemisphere to have longer days from March to September and shorter days in the other months.

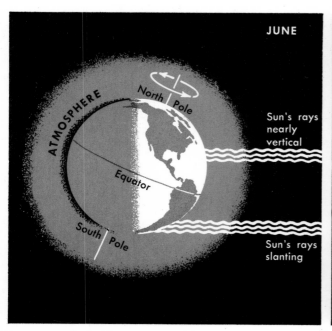

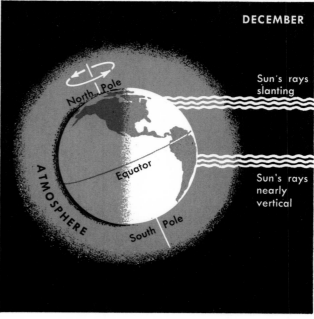

What makes the days
longer in summer and shorter in winter?

The 23½-degree tilt of the earth's axis not only causes a gradual change through the year in the warmth of the sun's rays, it also causes a change in the length of day and night. In the summer in the north the day is at its longest. In fact, at the North Pole there will be a time of "the midnight sun" with no sunset at all. The opposite will be true in winter, with no sunlight at all at the North Pole. While this is going on, the southern half of the world will be having seasons and amounts of daylight exactly opposite to that of the north.

In northern Alaska in the summer a baseball game isn't apt to be called on account of darkness. At the same time, in the Antarctic, scientists holed in at some camp in the ice will have nothing but a starry sky over their heads "day" after "day."

Why is it so cold
at the North and South Poles?

Our only important source of natural heat is the sun. In the far north or far south the rays of heat from the sun do not go directly through the atmosphere to the surface of the earth, as they do at the equator. The rays must go at a long, low angle through a great distance. Much of the heat in these rays is lost to the air on their relatively long journey, and some of the heat bounces back into space. Therefore, the lands at the poles are much colder than areas at the equator, so much colder that the ice in polar seas and the ice sheets on the land are found the year round. Temperatures of −125 degrees F., fierce winds, and the bleakness of expanses of white greet man at the poles. The Arctic Sea is more than 5,000,000 square miles in area, while Antarctica possesses 90 per cent of all of the earth's ice mass.

The world seems on fire as the sun slips below the horizon.

Why are sunsets red?

Travelogs of foreign lands always seem to end with a sunset shot. That magnificent sunset over the pyramids of Egypt, or the Statue of Liberty in New York, or even the beautiful, rosy-hued sunset seen from your own back yard, come from dust.

Ordinary sunlight appears as white light. In it are all the colors, but you usually don't see them unless they are broken down into a *spectrum,* as in a rainbow or a glass prism, which shows the full range of colors. With filters of different kinds you can allow only certain colors to be seen in light. Dust is a particular kind of filter that tends to favor the warm colors. The dust screens the visible light from the sun, allowing the red, orange, and yellow colors to get through at the expense of the other colors. This phenomena occurs when the sun's rays come toward us at a low angle, just before the sun disappears for the night.

What is the most
important source of heat in the world?

There is only one really important source of heat—the sun. Without the heat from the visible and invisible light of that brilliant star we would all be chilled to the bone, no matter what we tried to burn to keep warm. The absence of any heat at all would see temperatures dropping to *absolute zero* (—459 degrees F.), and without the sun everything would be almost that cold. Other sources of natural heat do not do much good.

What fuel is
the most plentiful on earth?

The almost complete change to diesel power for railroads and ships in recent years is not because of a greater natural abundance of oil compared to other fuels. Actually, there is more coal available in the ground than any other known substance suitable for supplying energy. Some scientists say that there may be some seven trillion tons of coal remaining in the ground.

The reasons for the shift to fuels other than coal have to do with convenience. In the case of oil, it is much easier to handle a liquid in closed tanks and to allow it to burn directly in an engine than it is to store a lumpy solid, feed it to a boiler, and heat a water supply to make steam. Further, the waste from a diesel engine goes into the air as exhaust. Burned coal leaves ashes which must be removed.

But this shouldn't lead one to think that coal is "out." On the contrary, the heat from coal still supplies more than half of all the electricity in the United States. Coal is an essential ingredient in iron and steel manufacture. Coal is rich in chemicals, and it supplies about one-third of all the United States' organic chemical industry with its raw material.

Geysers are thrilling things to watch.

Is there heat in the ground?

There is an increase in temperature directly related to depth in the ground. It has been demonstrated that the temperature under the surface of the earth rises from as much as one degree F. for every 30 feet of depth to about one degree F. in 250 feet. The average observation world-wide is about one degree F. in every 60 feet. At approximately 16,000 feet deep, an oil well in California showed a temperature of 400 degrees F.!

The source of this temperature increase seems to be twofold. One source is volcanic heat. This, of course, will raise temperatures locally to a great degree, and not just in the form of lava flowing from an eruption. Hot springs, geysers, mud pots, and other fascinating spectacles to be seen in such places as Yellowstone National Park are evidence enough. However, not all such effects can be considered as volcanic. Hot Springs, Virginia, has famous springs that are believed to be heated by the natural warmth generated in the crust of the earth by radioactive substances (uranium and thorium). Even in minute amounts these substances are enough to cause high temperatures within the material of the earth's crust.

All sources of heat other than the sun's do not add up to much, however, because they are masked by the insulation of the earth's crust. This crust—surface rocks, clay, water covered mostly, soil, etc.,—is a poor conductor of heat. Your feet wouldn't even be warm if the sun went on vacation.

How far out does the atmosphere go?

The air surrounding the earth is held against the planet by the pull of gravity. While the word "atmosphere" is defined in the dictionary as being nearly of the same meaning as "air," it is interesting to realize that science treats these terms a bit differently. Air is the mixture of gases which we breathe. It is densest at the surface of the earth. It thins rapidly with altitude, and at 75 or 100 miles there is so little that satellites can orbit for long periods of time without being slowed down very much by any friction from air.

But atmosphere means something more than just a mixture of gases dense enough to breathe or support an aircraft. Amounts of these gases, just barely enough to trace, plus a magnetic field stretching out in space from the earth's poles, combine to create a vast volume that is really the atmosphere of our planet. Man's knowledge of this is broadening all the time as space exploration develops sources of information. At the present time the atmosphere may be considered, for all practical purposes, as extending to about 200 miles altitude.

Two planes, 1,000 miles away from each other at points on the equator, fly true north at exactly the same speed. Do they ever meet?

They will meet at the North Pole. Although each will fly over a different route, their paths will gradually come together. Finally, though the planes were 1,000 miles apart at the start, they will come together right over the pole. Each of the planes will have flown the same number of miles when they meet. Take your globe and plot the course of these planes, and you can check this answer out.

Scientists have divided the atmosphere into parts and named them. The diagram at the right shows how far up the atmosphere has been penetrated by man and his satellites

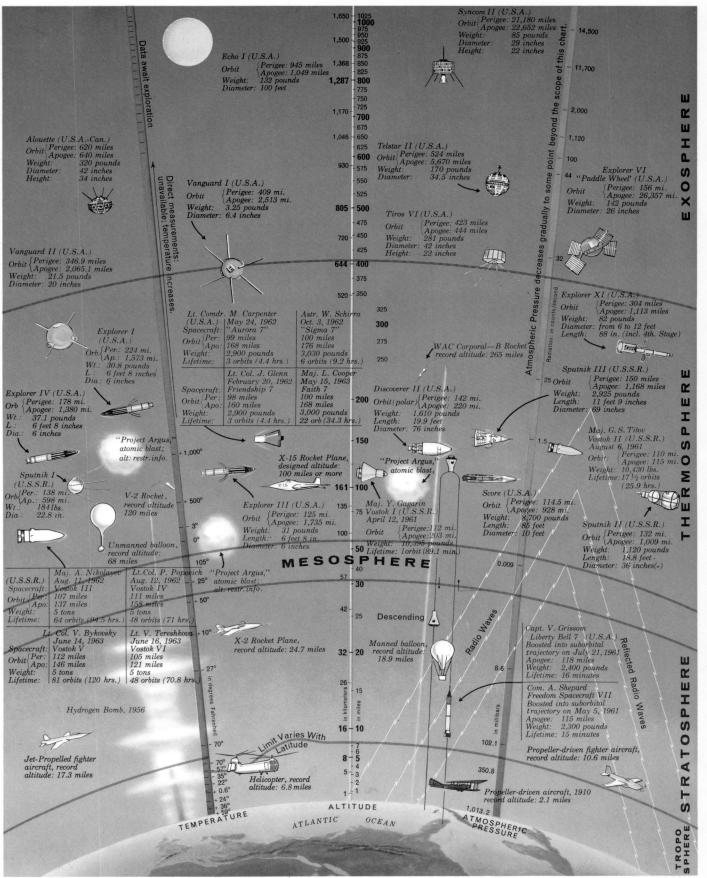

Syncom II (U.S.A.)
Orbit { Perigee: 21,180 miles / Apogee: 22,652 miles }
Weight: 85 pounds
Diameter: 29 inches
Height: 22 inches

Echo I (U.S.A.)
Orbit { Perigee: 945 miles / Apogee: 1,049 miles }
Weight: 132 pounds
Diameter: 100 feet

Data await exploration

Direct measurements unavailable; temperature increases.

Alouette (U.S.A.-Can.)
Orbit { Perigee: 620 miles / Apogee: 640 miles }
Weight: 320 pounds
Diameter: 42 inches
Height: 34 inches

Vanguard I (U.S.A.)
Orbit { Perigee: 409 mi. / Apogee: 2,513 mi. }
Weight: 3.25 pounds
Diameter: 6.4 inches

Telstar II (U.S.A.)
Orbit { Perigee: 524 miles / Apogee: 5,670 miles }
Weight: 170 pounds
Diameter: 34.5 inches

Atmospheric Pressure decreases gradually to some point beyond the scope of this chart.

Explorer VI "Paddle Wheel" (U.S.A.)
Orbit { Perigee: 156 mi. / Apogee: 26,357 mi. }
Weight: 142 pounds
Diameter: 26 inches

Vanguard II (U.S.A.)
Orbit { Perigee: 346.9 miles / Apogee: 2,065.1 miles }
Weight: 21.5 pounds
Diameter: 20 inches

Tiros VI (U.S.A.)
Orbit { Perigee: 423 miles / Apogee: 444 miles }
Weight: 281 pounds
Diameter: 42 inches
Height: 22 inches

Explorer XI (U.S.A.)
Orbit { Perigee: 304 miles / Apogee: 1,113 miles }
Weight: 82 pounds
Diameter: from 6 to 12 feet
Length: 88 in. (incl. 4th. Stage)

Explorer I (U.S.A.)
Orb. { Per.: 224 mi. / Ap.: 1,573 mi. }
Wt.: 30.8 pounds
L.: 6 feet 8 inches
Dia.: 6 inches

	Lt. Comdr. M. Carpenter (U.S.A.) May 24, 1962	Astr. W. Schirra Oct. 3, 1962
Spacecraft:	"Aurora 7"	"Sigma 7"
Orbit { Per. / Apo.	99 miles / 168 miles	100 miles / 176 miles
Weight:	2,900 pounds	3,030 pounds
Lifetime:	3 orbits (4.4 hrs.)	6 orbits (9.2 hrs.)
	Lt. Col. J. Glenn February 20, 1962	Maj. L. Cooper May 15, 1963
Spacecraft:	Friendship 7	Faith 7
Orbit { Per. / Apo.	98 miles / 160 miles	100 miles / 168 miles
Weight:	2,900 pounds	3,000 pounds
Lifetime:	3 orbits (4.4 hrs.)	22 orb (34.3 hrs.)

WAC Corporal—B Rocket record altitude: 265 miles

Sputnik III (U.S.S.R.)
Orbit { Perigee: 150 miles / Apogee: 1,168 miles }
Weight: 2,925 pounds
Length: 11 feet 9 inches
Diameter: 69 inches

Explorer IV (U.S.A.)
Orb { Perigee: 178 mi. / Apogee: 1,380 mi. }
Wt.: 37.1 pounds
L.: 6 feet 8 inches
Dia.: 6 inches

Discoverer II (U.S.A.)
Orbit (polar) { Perigee: 142 mi. / Apogee: 220 mi. }
Weight: 1,610 pounds
Length: 19.9 feet
Diameter: 76 inches

Maj. G. S. Titov
Vostok II
August 6, 1961
Orbit { Perigee: 110 mi. / Apogee: 115 mi. }
Weight: 10,430 lbs.
Lifetime: 17½ orbits (25.9 hrs.)

"Project Argus," atomic blast; alt: restr. info.

X-15 Rocket Plane, designed altitude: 100 miles or more

"Project Argus," atomic blast

Sputnik I (U.S.S.R.)
Orb { Per.: 138 mi. / Ap.: 598 mi. }
Wt.: 184 lbs.
Dia.: 22.8 in.

V-2 Rocket, record altitude 120 miles

Explorer III (U.S.A.)
Orbit { Perigee: 125 mi. / Apogee: 1,735 mi. }
Weight: 31 pounds
Length: 6 feet 8 in.
Diameter: 6 inches

Maj. Y. Gagarin
Vostok I (U.S.S.R.)
April 12, 1961
Orbit { Perigee: 112 mi. / Apogee: 203 mi. }
Weight: 10,395 pounds
Lifetime: 1 orbit (89.1 min.)

Score (U.S.A.)
Orbit { Perigee: 114.5 mi. / Apogee: 928 mi. }
Weight: 8,700 pounds
Length: 85 feet
Diameter: 10 feet

Sputnik II (U.S.S.R.)
Orbit { Perigee: 132 mi. / Apogee: 1,009 mi. }
Weight: 1,120 pounds
Length: 18.8 feet
Diameter: 36 inches(+)

Unmanned balloon, record altitude: 68 miles

(U.S.S.R.)	Maj. A. Nikolayev Aug. 11, 1962	Lt.Col. P. Popovich Aug. 12, 1962
Spacecraft:	Vostok III	Vostok IV
Orbit { Per. / Apo.	107 miles / 137 miles	111 miles / 158 miles
Weight:	5 tons	5 tons
Lifetime:	64 orbits (94.5 hrs.)	48 orbits (71 hrs.)
	Lt. Col. V. Bykovsky June 14, 1963	Lt. V. Tereshkova June 16, 1963
Spacecraft:	Vostok V	Vostok VI
Orbit { Per. / Apo.	112 miles / 146 miles	105 miles / 121 miles
Weight:	5 tons	5 tons
Lifetime:	81 orbits (120 hrs.)	48 orbits (70.8 hrs.)

"Project Argus," atomic blast; alt: restr. info.

MESOSPHERE

Descending

Manned balloon, record altitude: 18.9 miles

Radio Waves

Capt. V. Grissom Liberty Bell 7 (U.S.A.)
Boosted into suborbital trajectory on July 21, 1961
Apogee: 118 miles
Weight: 2,400 pounds
Lifetime: 16 minutes

Com. A. Shepard Freedom Spacecraft VII
Boosted into suborbital trajectory on May 5, 1961
Apogee: 115 miles
Weight: 2,300 pounds
Lifetime: 15 minutes

Hydrogen Bomb, 1956

X-2 Rocket Plane, record altitude: 24.7 miles

Reflected Radio Waves

Jet-Propelled fighter aircraft, record altitude: 17.3 miles

Limit Varies With Latitude

Helicopter, record altitude: 6.8 miles

in degrees Fahrenheit

Propeller-driven fighter aircraft, record altitude: 10.6 miles

Propeller-driven aircraft, 1910 record altitude: 2.1 miles

TEMPERATURE

ALTITUDE

ATLANTIC OCEAN

ATMOSPHERIC PRESSURE

in kilometers / *in miles*

in millibars

EXOSPHERE

THERMOSPHERE

STRATOSPHERE

TROPOSPHERE

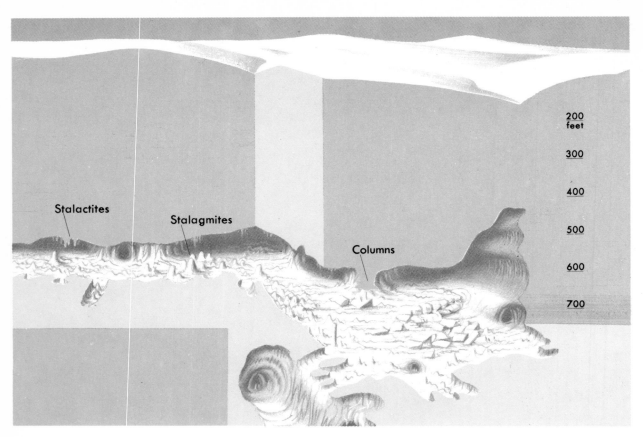

The Carlsbad Caverns are concealed deep in the earth of New Mexico.

Where is the world's deepest cave?

In southeastern France, near the city of Grenoble, is the Puits Berger cave system. This system is known to be at least 2,959 feet deep, and there have been reports of descents by speleologists—cave explorers—to more than 3,000 feet. There are estimates of even deeper caves in the French-Italian Alps, but so far there is no real proof.

The *largest* underground cavern in the world is in the United States. The Big Room in Carlsbad Caverns, New Mexico, measures 2,000 feet long, 285 feet high, and 1,100 feet wide. It is enormous, but this is size, not depth. Carlsbad is so far known to be only about 1,100 feet deep, not nearly so deep as the Puits Berger cave system.

In what fresh-water lake
are you apt to meet a shark?

In Lake Nicaragua there is a fresh-water species of shark that is known to have attacked man. The ancestors of this shark were probably trapped by a geological change such as the lowering of sea level, or the rising of the land, or both. Their sea home became a large pond when Lake Nicaragua was formed, and over succeeding years those of the species who were able to adapt to fresh water survived.

Sharks are known to other fresh water areas, also. The Ganges River in India, the Amazon in Brazil, and the Zambezi in Africa are only a few among many such locations.

The shark, one of the toughest creatures in existence, has ancestral lines going back about a hundred million years. It has managed to adapt itself to conditions that defeated almost all other animals who shared its earliest days.

What is the oldest inhabited city on earth?

History tells us of many cities founded before Damascus, Syria, but not one of them is inhabited today. Records show that the Aramaeans established Damascus at least before 1200 B.C., and that it became the seat of a kingdom of the same name.

The Aramaeans were the international traders of western Asia from 1100 B.C. to 500 B.C., and their language was the common tongue of many peoples. Damascus, with a population of about 530,000, is the largest city in Syria to this day. Although Egypt's history as an established civilization goes back farther into the past than the founding of Damascus, none of the centers which were the great names of ancient Egypt are functioning cities today.

What is the largest lake
in the United States?

Lake Michigan is the largest lake entirely within the borders of the U.S.A. The largest lake on the North American continent is Lake Superior, with 31,820 square miles, but it is shared geographically by Canada and the United States. Superior is also the largest fresh water lake in the world.

Man-made Lake Mead, formed by the Hoover Dam of the Colorado River, is 229 square miles in area, just about 1/100th the 22,400 square miles of Lake Michigan.

What in the world
is a seiche?

This is a peculiar kind of water-level variation occurring on lakes and bays, and it has even been known to happen along an ocean coast. Although it is not thoroughly understood, apparently it is the result of unequal wind and air-pressure forces on the surface of the water. The level of the water will rise enough to submerge docks and piers along a shore in a matter of minutes.

A seiche can be likened to the sloshing effect in a broad, shallow pan filled with water. Slight disturbances will set up an action that will cause the water to rise along the edge of the pan and run over.

Weather stations are learning how to predict seiches. Careful records of barometric pressure, temperature, and wind direction at the time of previous seiches have been noted. When these conditions recur, warnings are flashed over radio and television to give fishermen time to get off piers and boat owners time to take protective measures.

The rooftop of the world, the Himalayas.

Where in the world is the highest mountain range?

Separating the great Indian peninsula from the land mass of China and Russia to the north are the formidable Himalayas, stretching from West Pakistan to Burma. Here are twelve of the world's twenty highest mountains, at an over-all altitude above sea level greater than any locale on earth. Here, of course, is Everest, so long unassailed by man.

Politically, this is anything but certain territory. The name "Tibet" is at present fading from use because China decided that it would militarily consume that area, which slept for so many years atop the mountain heights. Kashmir is in dispute between India and Pakistan. Nepal, Sikkim, and Bhutan are threatened by China. The rooftop of the world may become a battleground.

Water from the Atlantic flows past the famous Rock of Gibraltar.

What becomes of all the water that flows as a great current into the Mediterranean Sea?

The Mediterranean is a warm sea under a subtropical sun with only one major tie to the open sea—the Strait of Gibraltar. The water in this basin is almost trapped, therefore. Why doesn't the sea overflow? A large part of the water evaporates into the warm air, and the large quantities coming in through the strait replenish the amount lost to the air. The evaporation also makes the surface water heavy with salt, which does not evaporate, and this heavy water sinks and flows out to the Atlantic at the bottom of the strait.

During World War II, submarines were known to coast in and out of the Mediterranean, with their electric motors off, by taking advantage of these two-way currents, upper level flow to go in, lower level to go out. Sound detection equipment of the Allies could not pick up any sign of the German submarines taking a quiet, free ride on the currents.

What great American city has a harbor with two "doors" 130 miles apart?

Coming in from the Atlantic Ocean, the largest ships in the world, such as the *Queen Mary* and the *United States,* can easily pass through Upper Bay and dock in the Hudson River alongside Manhattan Island in New York Harbor. Or, ships not quite so huge—though major vessels—can enter Long Island Sound 130 miles northeast and approach the city via the East River. As a bonus, the entire area is packed with rivers stretching far inland which are deep enough for navigation, and there are hundreds of bays, inlets, and coves. It is a sea captain's dream of a safe, snug harbor.

Why are most of the prominent cities of ancient times no longer "on the map"?

If the industry or occupation on which a city bases its life is no longer needed, or if its supply of materials is used up, the city may die. In modern Syria, you can see the ruins of the magnificent city of Palmyra, located where important trade routes crossed in ancient times. Then the caravans stopped using the routes. No one lives there now. The remains of the city stand alone and stark in the desert.

Political and economic reasons may see men forcing the death of a city by conquest. Carthage was the capital of an empire that challenged Rome's domination of the Mediterranean Sea hundreds of years before Christ. Carthage was the land of the famous Hannibal, the great general who took elephants on a military expedition on the European continent and crossed the Alps with these beasts. The Carthaginians were a thorn in the sides of the Romans, who did not relish the prosperity and power of their rivals just across the narrowest part of the Mediterranean. Battles were fought time and time again. Finally the Romans decided to defeat Carthage once and for all. They assaulted the great city and virtually destroyed it in 146 B.C. Carthage never recovered to any degree. You can see what is left of it today in the country of Tunisia, near the city of Tunis.

History is packed with records of "lost" cities whose end came from changes in the patterns of their economic life, climatic change, exhaustion of natural resources, and the ravages of war. Military conquest has deprived the world of some of its most glorious, vital civilizations.

Time stopped for this ancient city in the morning, 79 A.D.

Where in the world can you see an ancient city as it was on the day when a volcano buried it in ashes?

A medium-sized city of about 20,000 persons, Pompeii was a fine example of a typical Roman community. It was prosperous, and while it did have some evil ways, there was nothing especially wrong with its manner of life. Homes, temples, theaters, stadium, baths, many of them superb examples of architecture, were surrounded by a wall with at least eight gates. In 62 A.D. the town suffered a serious earthquake, not unusual for shock-prone Italy, and the townspeople proceeded to repair the damage. The quake was a straw in the wind, but the residents did not realize it. Nearby Monte Somma, while known to be a volcano, was thought to be extinct.

In 79 A.D. Monte Somma changed. Violent explosions blew its mass toward the sea, and toward Pompeii, catching the town in its tracks. The life of Pompeii was snuffed out and yet it was captured intact forever. The rain of ashes trapped people where they stood and even enveloped the details of daily life just as they were at the moment. The town was buried in twelve feet of volcanic ash, buried so well, in fact, that its site was lost to records until canal diggers in 1748 ran into traces of Pompeii's magnificent buildings.

Excavation has been underway ever since. Though not, even today, completely cleared of its debris, Pompeii may now be seen as a permanently preserved example of a Roman Empire city at the time of Christ. Somma's crater at the time of the explosion gave birth to the volcanic cone known as Vesuvius, which is now 3,842 feet high.

Where in the world is the country that changed continents?

Panama is considered today to be geographically a part of Central and North America. Yet its history has a South American background.

Originally, Panama was included in Spanish territory as part of the Viceroyalty of Peru. Then, in 1718, it was joined to New Granada. During later revolts against Spanish rule, Panama remained attached to Colombia, which is clearly a part of the South American continent. While the territory enjoyed some freedom from Colombia, from 1885 to 1903 it was ruled from Bogotá, capital of Colombia.

A revolution in 1903 gave Panama its independence from Colombia. With its political connection to South America severed, Panama "changed" continents and attached itself to North America.

Why do ships have to go through the Netherlands to dock at Belgium's main port?

A sea coast does not necessarily mean that there will be good ports. Belgium's North Sea coast is relatively straight and smooth, and there are no great natural harbor areas. Immediately to the north, the Netherlands coast is broken with numerous inlets and land areas reclaimed from the sea. Antwerp, Belgium's principal port city, is reached by sailing from the North Sea through Dutch territory into the Schelde River.

Where in the United States do you find
skeletons of sabre-tooth tigers and camels?

On Wilshire Boulevard in Los Angeles the city has landscaped a park and erected a museum building on the site of the "fossil pits." You can look at the pits from modern buildings nearby, or wander through paths built in the park and see statues of sabre-tooth tigers, camels, and other creatures that lived in prehistoric times. The actual skeletons turned into fossils by ages of chemical action were found preserved in pools of tar, and are now in the Los Angeles Museum.

Where in the world are diamonds found?

In quantities great enough to support the large organized effort of mining, Africa is alone in its natural supply of diamonds.

Diamonds are believed to have been formed under conditions of great heat, about 5,000 degrees F., and the pressure of 1,000,000 pounds per square inch deep inside the earth's crust, perhaps 250 miles down. Pure carbon was, under these conditions, transformed into the hardest of materials, the beautiful, clear substance that is so treasured around the world.

Magma—the fluid rock that underlies the solid crust of the earth—brought these diamonds to the surface in volcanic eruptions. In the outlet for the gases and lava—the pipe—of now extinct and cool volcanoes, diamonds are found today. Kimberlite, a bluish rock found in the pipe, is the prime source, and it was the discovery of numbers of these pipes that brought wealth from diamonds to Kimberley, Pretoria, and other African locations.

Not all mining of diamonds is in pipes, however. Erosion at diamond-bearing rock may result in diamonds being found some distance away from the volcanic source. Water washing the ground away may carry the soil and diamonds far from the original location. Diamonds in some quantity have been "mined" in Brazil and India from these sources.

Glacial deposits in Wisconsin, Michigan, Ohio, and Indiana also have been found to have diamonds. Presumably a source far north in Canada—as yet undiscovered—was tapped by the Ice Age glaciers, and diamonds were carried by the ice sheets as they moved south. The only significant source of diamonds in the United States, however, is in the state of Arkansas.

What country has pushed back the sea?

Look at a map of the Netherlands and you will see that much of the western part of the country is below sea level. Since Columbus' time the Dutch have been inching their land out into the water, and areas below the surface of the North Sea have been added to their country. By building dikes in shallow seas, and then pumping the sea water out, they have made land out of sea bottom. This land is called a "polder." In time the saltiness of the ocean is washed out of the bottom soil, and it can be used for farming, grazing, and the building of villages. More than four thousand square miles of the Netherlands were formerly under the surface of the sea.

Land that was once the sea.

What is the largest state
in the United States east of the Mississippi?

Georgia with a land area of 58,274 square miles is the largest state east of the Mississippi. Its total land and water area is 58,876 square miles, still keeping it slightly ahead of Florida which has a land area of 54,252 square miles, a water area of 4,308 square miles, and a total area of 58,560 square miles.

What state in the United States
is the highest above sea level?

Colorado is, on the average, 6,800 feet above sea level, and has 49 mountains that are over 14,000 feet high. The highest point is Mt. Elbert, at 14,431 feet, while the lowest point, at 3,350 feet, is at Prowers on the Arkansas River.

It is interesting that Colorado's capital city, Denver, is exactly one mile above sea level; 5,280 feet, no more, no less.

What is one of the loneliest spots on earth?

Tristan da Cunha, in the South Atlantic, is more than 1,300 miles from the nearest inhabited island of St. Helena, and 1,700 miles from South Africa, the nearest continent. It is a tiny island on which about 250 people live.

Extreme volcanic activity recently forced these inhabitants to seek refuge in the British Isles. Most of them did not enjoy their stay with civilization, and now that the volcano seems to be quiet again, they have chosen to return to their home, away from the luxuries—and problems—of the mechanical age.

Are diamonds mined primarily for jewelry?

The importance of diamonds does not lie in their use as gems in rings or necklaces. About 80 per cent of diamonds that are processed go into industrial use. Because of their great hardness, diamonds are used in large quantities by industry for cutting, grinding, and polishing metals and other materials.

Diamonds are so useful, for example, that a diamond-dust-coated drill bit used to cut a two-inch hole in concrete will cost over one hundred dollars. Yet, such a drill allows the cut to be made so much faster and more efficiently than with ordinary steel drilling materials that it easily pays for itself in use.

When did the soil of the United States' Southwest darken the sky of the Atlantic coast?

During the 1930's it was fairly common for an Easterner, waking in the morning, to see a thick layer of dust covering his furniture, and to note sunlight made red and dim by a sky loaded with dust.

This dust was soil that had blown all the way across the United States from the "dust bowl" of southwestern United States. There the people had plowed and planted the soil in a climate that was too dry to give good crops year after year. Erosion and drought caused the soil to blow away in the wind. The area has since been returned mostly to grazing land—its natural state.

Has man explored the highest and lowest points on earth?

As far as man knows, probably. Mt. Everest, the highest of mountains at 29,028 feet, was scaled in 1953 by Sir Edmund Hillary and Tenzing Norgay. In 1960 the bathyscaphe *Trieste,* with Jacques Piccard and Lt. Don Walsh aboard, went down to 35,640 feet in the Marianas Trench south of Guam in the Pacific Ocean, then thought to be the deepest point of the ocean. Published reports of soundings indicate that other points in the Marianas Trench may be 500 feet deeper.

Exploration at these extremes is a rather limited thing, however. Hillary and Tenzing were not free to spend an extended period walking around on Everest's top. The conditions of altitude, cold, burdensome clothing, and snow did not allow much exploring. Even more restrictive was the use of the bathyscaphe, a vessel capable of only very limited movement. The men inside were strictly confined to the interior, peering out through a small porthole. As a beginning, it can be said that they were at least physically present where no other man has ever been.

Is mountain climbing an ancient custom?

Not much mountain climbing was done before the fifteenth century, and it wasn't until about 1850 that it began to catch on as a popular sport. People used to believe that mountains were the homes of gods who would be offended by anyone climbing to their peaks, or they looked upon the towering rock as some sort of obstacle that was a big bother.

Edward Whymper, an artist who was sent off to the Alps by a London publisher to sketch, became so fascinated by mountain climbing that he was the first to conquer the famous Matterhorn of Switzerland, 14,685 feet, in 1865. Mt. Whitney, 14,495 feet, the highest mountain in the

United States before Alaska was annexed, was first climbed in 1873. Mt. McKinley, 20,320 feet, the highest mountain on the North American continent, in Alaska, was first climbed in 1913.

Where in the world is the tallest mountain?

Mt. Everest, at 29,028 feet, is the mountain that is the highest above sea level, of course. However, Mauna Kea, on the island of Hawaii, is the tallest mountain measured from its base. From the immediately surrounding ocean floor where its base lies, Mauna Kea rises about 17,000 feet from *below* sea level to 13,796 feet *above* sea level, a total of over 30,000 feet. Its companion, the famous Mauna Loa, is 13,680 feet above sea level, and it too has its base on the floor of the ocean. The mountains of volcanic islands may have a claim to even more impressive statistics.

What famous ship is supposed to have ended its voyage on top of a mountain?

The highest mountain in Turkey, Mt. Ararat (16,946 feet) is said by some to be the final dry dock that *Noah's Ark* of the Bible found at the end of the Great Flood. Although there have been reports that traces of such a ship have been sighted there, careful thinkers are awaiting more complete information.

Did the voyage end here?

Can a barometer be used
to determine
the height of land features?

It certainly can. A barometer is an instrument used to measure atmospheric pressure, and atmospheric pressure varies with the height of land above sea level. At sea level, the normal barometric pressure is 29.92 inches; at 1,000 feet, the pressure drops to 28.86 inches; at 2,000 feet, 27.82 inches; and at 3,000 feet, 26.81 inches.

Most barometers have a hand pointing to a scale (dial) indicating the pressure. If you change the scale to read in feet, you have an altimeter, an instrument used to indicate height about sea level, measured on the basis of the difference in atmospheric pressure. If, knowing the difference in normal barometric pressure at different heights, you convert the barometric reading in inches to feet, you have a means of "surveying" the land surface while carrying the barometer, thus estimating height quite well.

Where is the world's
longest natural bridge
and how was it formed?

The Landscape Arch in Arches National Monument, Utah, is the longest, measuring 291 feet. About one hundred feet above the canyon floor, Landscape Arch has been cut by nature to a mere six-foot thickness at its narrowest section.

Although this bridge and many other natural wonders are frequently described as being the product of wind erosion, other factors usually play a more important part in their creation. The seepage of water into the rock, followed by quick freezing, will cause the surface to flake and fall off. Additional rock falls will be caused by the weathering of rain, drought, heat and cold, continuing nature's process of sculpting odd shapes. Wind erosion, the abrasion by particles of sand, will contribute then to the molding.

What was Columbus doing in Iceland?

Christopher Columbus was a first-rate seagoing man—a navigator with an uncanny sense of the right thing to do, and a sailor with extensive experience. Shipping as a common sailor, he learned the skills of sailing on a variety of voyages, one of which took him to Iceland.

Samuel Eliot Morison tells, in *Admiral of the Ocean Sea,* how in 1477 Columbus, then twenty-five, went on one of his adventurous voyages that seasoned him as a man of varied sea background. He shipped out on a voyage that was part of the trade of that time between Lisbon, Portugal, the Azores, Bristol, England, and Iceland. Columbus' notes on the voyage refer to ". . . a hundred leagues beyond the island of Tile, whose northern part is in Latitude 73 degrees North and not 63 degrees, as some would have it be . . . [The captain and/or Columbus were wrong here; it is 63 degrees.] . . . to this island, which is as big as England, come English with their merchandise, especially they of Bristol. And at the season when I was there the sea was not frozen. . . ."

Columbus' biographers point to this as proof that the great navigator had gone at least as far as Iceland (Tile); this is certain. Columbus' reference to a hundred leagues *beyond* Tile introduces the intriguing thought that he saw even farther territory. A league was about three miles, and three hundred miles beyond Iceland is approximately the distance to Greenland. In any case, Columbus was a seasoned voyager by the year 1492.

How many different ways are there to draw a map?

Our earth is shaped like a ball, and the best way to portray it is to copy it in miniature. The familiar globe is the result, a true picture of the surface of earth, with its land and water. But since it is hard to put a globe in a notebook or carry it in your pocket, we have maps, pictures of the globe on flat paper.

It's quite difficult to accurately represent the features of a curved surface on a flat piece of paper. Men have been working on the problem of flattening the globe for many years, developing numerous methods. In the process, though, one or more of the true features of the globe is lost. Distance, or relative size and shape of features, or directions will no longer be true.

For example, let's pretend to make a map. Imagine a glass globe with some of the features of earth marked on its surface. A lighted bulb is placed inside at the center. A cylindrical roll of paper is placed around the glass globe. The light rays shine through the glass and make shadow lines on the paper. Where the features of the globe show on the paper they are marked with ink or pencil. Remove the paper and flatten it and you have a map of the world, complete except for the far north and south; it is impossible to catch light rays coming through the poles.

This map would be *similar* to a Mercator projection, and would be true for north-south or east-west directions, but not for directions in between. Distortion of features far north or south would be great. Greenland, for instance, would appear many times its actual relative size.

At the beginning of the Age of Discovery, sailors used charts that were good for travel near homelands only. In these latitudes directions and distances were almost true. But the long voyages of such explorers as Columbus could not be plotted as a straight line. In 1569, Mercator worked out a system that overcame this problem with charts that were accurate for any compass direction. While areas far north or south were exaggerated in size, small areas were true in shape.

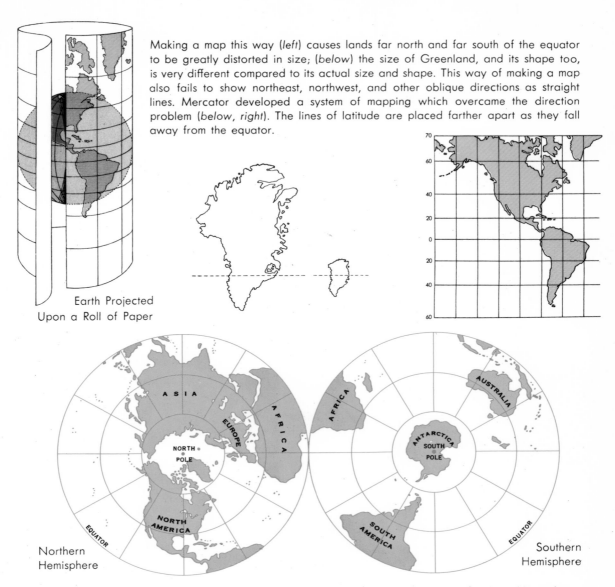

Making a map this way (*left*) causes lands far north and far south of the equator to be greatly distorted in size; (*below*) the size of Greenland, and its shape too, is very different compared to its actual size and shape. This way of making a map also fails to show northeast, northwest, and other oblique directions as straight lines. Mercator developed a system of mapping which overcame the direction problem (*below, right*). The lines of latitude are placed farther apart as they fall away from the equator.

Earth Projected
Upon a Roll of Paper

Northern
Hemisphere

Southern
Hemisphere

A useful map in the jet age is made by showing the lands of the Northern and Southern Hemispheres grouped around their respective poles. This kind of map is sometimes called a polar projection.

Mercator's charts were not made with a glass globe and cylinder. He plotted the location of features on his charts to overcome the direction problem. But the basic principles of map projection can be gained from visualizing the glass globe idea. There have been many projections developed through the years, conic, equal-area, gnomonic, etc. There are as many ways to draw maps as there are needs for them, from the wall map in a classroom to the road map in the family car.

Why does it rain?

All air normally contains some moisture. The amount of moisture air can hold depends on its temperature. This moisture contained in the air is not visible, like fog or rain; rather, it is held as a vapor, an invisible gas. A certain amount of air at a particular temperature will hold just so much of this water vapor. If the temperature is raised, the air can hold more water. Lowering the temperature of air which has as much moisture as it can contain will cause condensation—that is, the vapor becomes droplets of water which you can see.

This is what happens in the summer when the outer surface of a glass containing an iced drink becomes wet. Air touching the surface of the glass becomes chilled enough to release the moisture it contains. The temperature at which air releases its water vapor in condensed form is called the *dew point*.

Basically, this is what happens in the formation of fog and clouds and when it rains. Fog forms when the dew point is reached at the level of the ground; clouds are formed when the dew point is reached higher in the air. Rain is simply condensation on a larger scale. The tiny droplets of moisture one finds in fog or clouds join together, in the case of rain, and fall to earth as large drops of water.

Raindrops form under many different circumstances. One familiar one is when warm, moist air is forced to rise over a mountain range. Another is when a warm, moist air mass meets a cold air mass and is cooled to the dew point or below.

THE FORMATION OF RAIN

COLD DOWNDRAFT

WARM UPDRAFT

COLD HEAVY AIR

Over mountains   By convection   Over heavy air

Mt. Kilimanjaro

Why are some mountains snow capped?

Wind is forced to climb to pass over a mountain. In so doing its make-up changes. Higher altitudes mean lower atmospheric pressure and colder temperatures. The moisture in the wind is forced out as it contracts and cools below its "dew point," causing rain, or if the temperatures are cold enough, snow. The lower sustained temperatures of the mountains' heights preserve the snow. Even mountains located on the equator, if high enough, will be snow capped. Mt. Kilimanjaro in Tanganyika near the border of Kenya-in Africa is snow covered.

Where has it never rained?

In the Atacama desert region in Chile there has been no really significant rainfall recorded in at least 400 years. Arica, up the Chilean coast, had a record of an average of .02 inches of rain per year for over 40 years. Oddly enough, Chile seems also to have the record for the area in which rain occurs most frequently. At Bahía Felix to the south, it rains, on the average, 325 days a year, and in 1916, rain fell on 348 of the 366 days.

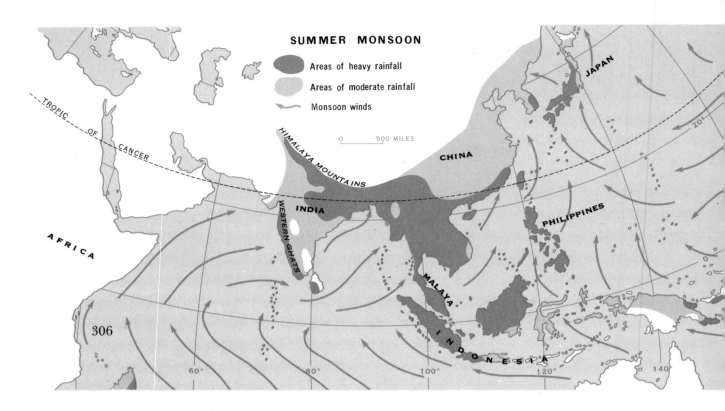

Large areas of Asia are drenched by annual monsoons.

What is a monsoon?

The southern part of the huge land mass of Asia experiences great heat from the sun in late spring and early summer. The air rises as it is heated, and warm, moist winds move in from the Indian and Pacific Oceans to take its place. As the air passes over the higher land masses and the mountains, it releases rainfall greater than anywhere else on earth.

The monsoon (from an Arabic word meaning "season") is a weather condition of extreme, torrential rain that spreads over India, China, Japan, Malaya, the Philippines, and Indonesia. The monsoon is the great provider of water which makes it possible for these lands to feed and clothe their great populations. Farmers formerly could make use of the water brought to the land by these summer rains only during the rainy season and for a short time afterward. Now the water not used immediately is stored and feeds irrigation systems for as long as it can be made to last.

What's the hardest it's ever rained?

Because there are no weather stations in so many parts of the world, there is no way of knowing if official records really represent the greatest amounts of rainfall. These records are, however, startling enough.

Most intense rainfall rate: .69 inch in one minute at Jefferson, Iowa, on July 10, 1955.

Greatest amount in 24 hours in the United States: 23.22 inches in New Smyrna, Florida, on October 10–11, 1924.

Greatest in one month in the world: 366.14 inches at Cherrapunji, Assam, India, in July, 1861.

Greatest in one year in the world: 1,041.78 inches again at Cherrapunji, Assam, India, from August 1, 1860 to July 31, 1861.

The average annual rainfall at Cherrapunji is 450 inches, ample evidence of the influence of the monsoon on Asian climate. But the greatest annual average of rainfall in the world is in the fiftieth state, at Mt. Waialeale on Kauai, Hawaii, where a yearly average of 460 inches has fallen since 1912.

Where are there people living today who are as primitive as the people of the Stone Age?

In Australia the Bindibu aborigines live in the bleak west-central desert under conditions that even some Stone-Agers would probably have found quite primitive. They have no utensils to hold water for drinking (they drink water as animals do, lapping it up), wear no clothes, raise no crops, do not have homes, and have no art. They dig for food in the ground with sticks, and hunt with a kind of boomerang. They have an unbelievable ability to live under conditions that most people in the world would find unbearable.

Where in the world is the greatest waterfall?

It depends on what is meant by "greatest." Angel Falls in Venezuela has a total drop of 3,312 feet, a fall of about 900 feet more than the Upper and Lower Yosemite Falls together. The waterfall with the greatest flow of water is said to be the Guaíra in Brazil. Its flow, at 470,000 cubic feet per second, is over twice that of Niagara Falls.

What makes Niagara Falls so famous?

Niagara's fame is not due to the height or flow of water. The falls are famous first because they are a beautiful sight, easily reached by millions of people who live on the North American continent. The water of the Niagara River cascades 167 feet in two major cataracts, the American Falls and the Canadian Falls. These cataracts measure across about 1,000 and 2,500 feet, respectively. The total width of Niagara Falls is about 3,500 feet. Even this tremendous width does not make Niagara the waterfall with the longest edge. Victoria Falls of the Zambezi River in Africa claim this honor, with a total length of more than one mile, broken into three major cataracts. But Victoria Falls lie in a remote area.

Niagara is also famous because it is a key part of a water system that is one of the most interesting in the world—the Great Lakes. These lakes, starting at Lake Superior over a thousand miles inland, followed by Michigan, Huron, Erie, and Ontario in turn, are a vast reservoir of water that spills, like a series of giant pans, one into the other.

The water is first gathered from rivers, springs, rain, and snow at 602 feet above sea level in Lake Superior. From here it goes into Lake Michigan (which is really a huge bay) and Lake Huron, both at 580 feet above sea level, and then into Lake Erie at 572 feet above sea level. From Lake Erie the water goes into the Niagara River, dropping down

VICTORIA FALLS

YOSEMITE FALLS

NIAGARA FALLS

ANGEL FALLS

Waterfalls are beautiful, and if they are close to man's choice of home, sometimes he can harness the power they generate and make them work for him.

the river, including the 167 feet over the falls, into Lake Ontario at 246 feet. Ontario drains into the St. Lawrence River, where the water drops gradually to the level of the ocean at the Gulf of St. Lawrence. With what amounts to an immense river whose scale challenges comparison, North America has a tremendous water supply, half of the fresh water in the world.

How much water do you need a day?

You may drink only a few glasses of water a day, but if you are an average American you use about 1,700 gallons each 24 hours! All of this quantity you may not use directly, but this amount is necessary for you in the twentieth-century pattern of living. You and your family use water to bathe, wash, cook, and dispose of wastes. But you also have refrigerators and stoves, use medicines, wear manufactured clothes, have a car and burn gasoline, have an oil burner and burn oil, build with processed lumber, paint your house, eat prepared foods, read newspapers and books, and buy almost everything packaged.

Every one of these things, and many more, consumes water in fantastic quantities in the manufacture and handling. It takes, for example, 250 tons of water to make one ton of paper, 10,000 tons of water to grow one ton of cotton.

Where is there a depression in the earth's surface that is more than 1,286 feet below sea level?

The Dead Sea, shared by Israel and Jordan, is a stopped-up reservoir that lies about one-quarter of a mile lower than the level of the Mediterranean Sea, which is only about fifty miles west. The shores of the Dead Sea are recognized as the lowest point of land in the world.

Because the reservoir is so far below sea level, the only way it loses water is by evaporation. This leaves heavy concentrations of salts in its waters and makes it possible for the Israeli to extract commercial quantities of potash and bromides.

The extent of ancient shores in Utah.

What great lake is disappearing before our eyes?

Great Salt Lake in Utah is going down so fast that beach houses and piers built not many years ago are now high and dry. You can see terraces, once the shore line, now 1,000 feet above the surface.

The grandfather to this lake, called Lake Bonneville, covered an area as large as today's Lake Michigan. In prehistoric times, as now, the amount of water flowing in failed to strike a balance with the amount evaporating and draining out, and the level of water has been dropping ever since.

Before too many more years people will no longer be able to enjoy a very odd experience at this famous lake—floating like a cork when going for a swim. Due to the heavy concentration of salt, the water is much more buoyant—heavier—than fresh water, or even sea water, and you can float around with your head and feet out of the water.

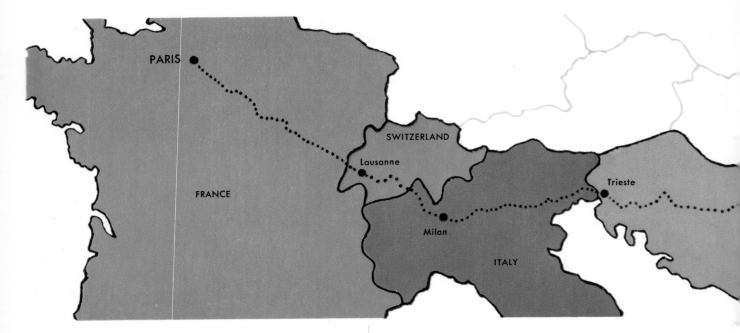

What train from Paris ends its run
in a city located on two continents?

The Simplon-Orient Express, a train that has inspired many spy and murder mystery stories of both book and motion picture fame, begins its run in Paris and crosses seven countries' borders. It travels through France and Switzerland, through the Simplon Tunnel (more than 12 miles in length, opened in 1905), into and across Italy, through Yugoslavia, Bulgaria, across a small section of Greece, and finally into Turkey. The Simplon-Orient Express then travels across Turkish soil and ends its run in Istanbul, the former Constantinople, known in ancient times as Byzantium. Istanbul, located on both sides of the Bosporus Strait, the narrow connection between the Black Sea and the waters leading to the Mediterranean, is the gateway to Asia. Its western portion lies in European Turkey; its eastern part across the strait in Asian Turkey. (Actually 90 per cent of Turkey's land is in Asia.)

The Orient Express is a remarkable example of international co-operation. It once deserved its reputation as the carrier of mysterious persons on errands of international intrigue, for it does travel through nations that have been both allies and enemies at various times. In its prime, the Orient Express was a valuable and swift means of travel for

A connection from the heart of Europe to the door of Asia.

businessmen, diplomatic couriers, tourists, and, no doubt, spies. Today, trains usually are displaced by planes as the common carriers of persons on missions. Still, the Simplon-Orient Express continues to travel on rails that directly connect the vastly different cities of Paris and Istanbul, spanning 1,400 miles to join the heart of Europe to the door to Asia.

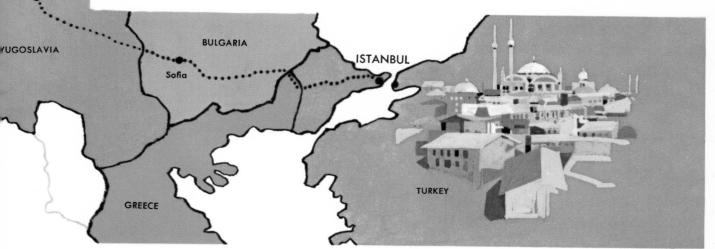

What country has the world's largest railway system?

The United States has over 215,000 miles of railroad lines, the greatest for any country. This is equal to about one mile of railway for every 12 square miles of area.

Belgium has more railroad track for its size than any country—one mile of track for about 1.5 square miles. British railways carry more people than any other system, but the Japanese State Railway System gets the honors for the greatest number of passenger miles.

The importance of the railroad to the United States becomes clear when freight is considered. Freight movement on U.S. railroads is the greatest on earth, and the volume of cargo handled is far greater than that handled by any other method of transportation, city to city. The two billion tons of freight hauled by the railroads each year require 1,550,000 freight cars!

Is our planet the largest planet in our solar system?

Earth's mean diameter of 7,918 miles ranks it fifth in any contest for size. Compared with the other planets, it is smaller than Jupiter, Saturn, Uranus, and Neptune, but larger than Venus, Mars, Pluto, and Mercury. Jupiter is ten times bigger than our planet.

What was the first earth satellite?

It is still in orbit. It can be seen in a roughly equatorial orbit, passing once around the earth every approximately 28 days. Its altitude is about 239,000 miles, and it is about 2,160 miles in diameter. It was placed in orbit about 5,000,000,000 years ago. It is the moon.

Why are there tides in the oceans?

The sun and the moon have an attraction similar to the force of gravity, and the level of the water that covers most of the earth is literally shifted back and forth by the pull of these bodies far out in space. Because the world's water has an irregular shore line of land, with bays, peninsulas, and partially enclosed seas of differing depth, the oceans will not rise or fall evenly as the sun and moon pull on their waters. According to the position of the sun and moon, the water will flow in and out at different rates, called spring tides or neap tides.

Over the great areas of the oceans, the tide will rise and fall without notice in mid-ocean, and a ship will calmly proceed as if nothing had happened. At the same time, along a shore the water will be stolen away for a while at low or ebb tide and come flowing back in at high or flood tide. There is great variance in tidal patterns, world-wide, but the normal schedule is for two high tides and two low tides for every twenty-four hours, approximately. Some places have only one high and one low tide a day (along the Gulf of Mexico in certain areas), and the schedule will change according to a complicated pattern.

When are there eclipses?

There are two kinds of eclipses commonly known to man—one of the moon, another of the sun. Eclipses of the moon are more frequent than eclipses of the sun, and they occur when the earth's orbit around the sun (the ecliptic) puts it between the sun and its natural satellite during the full-moon phase. At this time the moon usually appears dull red due to the deflection of the sun's rays by the atmosphere that envelops the whole earth.

The sun may be partly shadowed in certain portions of the earth when the new moon's orbit places it between the sun and the earth. This is a partial eclipse and it is seen in those areas that fall under the wide-angle shadow of the moon, what scientists call the *penumbra*. A total eclipse of the sun occurs only in those places on earth which lie in the *umbra,* the direct shadow cast by the new moon on the earth.

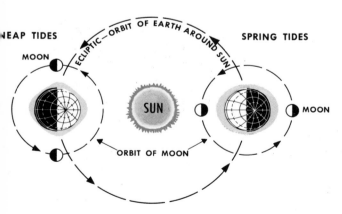

The moon's attraction in its first and third quarters works against that of the sun and the range of tides decreases; then high tide is called neap tide. In its full and new phase, the moon's attraction works with that of the sun, the tides increase in range and are called spring tides.

An eclipse of the moon occurs when the earth comes between the moon and the sun during a full moon. An eclipse of the sun occurs when the moon passes between the earth and the sun during a new moon. A total eclipse can be seen only where the earth is shadowed by the moon, in the umbra.

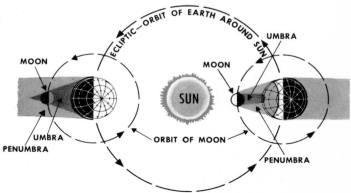

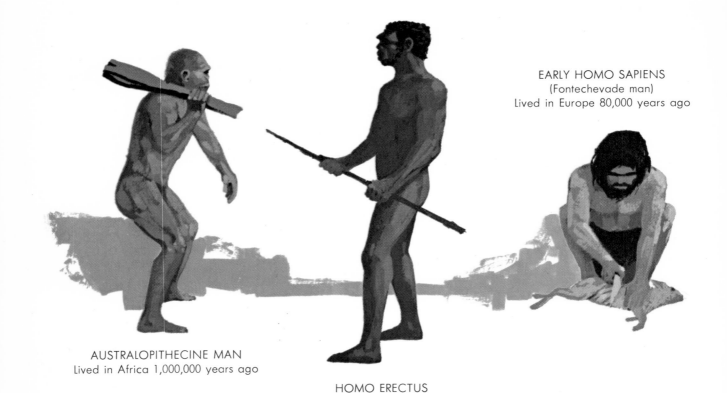

EARLY HOMO SAPIENS
(Fontechevade man)
Lived in Europe 80,000 years ago

AUSTRALOPITHECINE MAN
Lived in Africa 1,000,000 years ago

HOMO ERECTUS
Lived in Asia 300,000 years ago

LATER HOMO SAPIENS
(Rhodesian man)
Lived in Africa 40,000 years ago

NEANDERTHAL MAN
Lived in Europe 37,000 years ago

Where in the world did people first live?

The search for a positive answer to this question is the greatest whodunit of all. Archaeologists and paleontologists are like detectives who arrive on the scene five thousand or five-hundred-thousand years late. They must piece together tiny fragments of clues that have been buried by countless accidents of nature, floods, and the accumulated debris of succeeding civilizations. The bits and pieces of a culture may lie at the bottom of a pile of rubbish left by numerous others. Man often builds on top of what those before him built and left. The city of Rome is a prime example of this habit of man.

The detective work is especially complicated by the fact that man (Homo sapiens) was on earth before some primitive man-apes and earlier man-types faded out. Neanderthal man—the cave man—was flourishing over much of the old world at the same time as Homo sapiens.

At present, evidence points to Homo sapiens being alive perhaps one-hundred-thousand years ago and to early man-types first emerging at least as long ago as one million years somewhere on the continent of Africa. In 1932 at a site near the northeast corner of Lake Victoria, in Kenya, the paleontologist Louis Leakey found fossil fragments believed to be human and perhaps a million years old. Recently Leakey found fossil parts of even earlier creatures in the Olduvai Gorge of Tanganyika. These were Homo habilis in type, who stood 3½ to 4½ feet tall and are thought to have lived in the gorge area 1,820,000 years ago.

While early ape-man and early man-type fossils are found in many other parts of the world, Africa possesses more evidence that early man, or proto-man, originated there. No one, of course, knows why or how. Evolution teaches us, however, that an early type of ape may have found itself forced into circumstances where only some unusual members of its species survived. Perhaps only those who could walk erect, and use sticks and stones as weapons, consistently lived through a climatic change. The apes which adapted may have become an early proto-man.

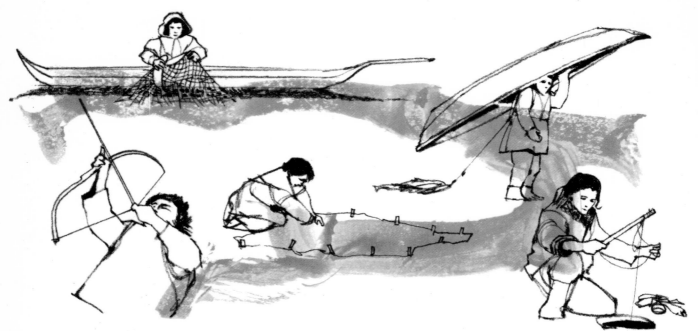

The Canadian Eskimos hunt and fish and make their clothes from hides.

Can man live anywhere in the world?

Man's choice of a home is influenced to a great extent by conditions of terrain, climate, food, mineral deposits, and water supply. Yet man seems to be able to defy unsatisfactory conditions and still survive. The Eskimos are a good example. They live in a most inhospitable part of the world. Winters are long, summers brief, there is no abundance of a variety of foods. Meat and fish, much of which would be considered inedible by other people, comprise the bulk of the diet.

Why do Eskimos live in the cold far north? For one thing, there are not many Eskimos. The population is just about in balance with the harsh surroundings and meager resources. Another factor is that the Eskimo people are adjusted to their surroundings and their diet, and through the years these hardy souls have survived and have had hardy children.

Man can live anywhere on earth if he adjusts his way of living with equipment suited to the region. But the ice cap of the Antarctic and the scorching rock beds of the desert are forbidding. The largest groups of people will be found where water and food supplies are in abundance, where natural resources provide opportunities for trade and manufacture.

74

Can we "farm" the seas?

Men have been sea hunters for a long time. A fisherman does not usually reap a harvest based on an organized plan of breeding. He is taking from the sea without providing for replenishment.

Some steps have been taken in the direction of planning. Oyster farms are areas where fences have been placed in the water to keep the enemies of the oyster away. Pearls are "farmed" from carefully organized beds offshore in Japan. There are places in the orient where fish are grown in fresh-water ponds on a large scale. Fish hatcheries in the United States are commonly employed to stock ponds and lakes for the benefit of the balance of nature and for fishermen. Seaweed is harvested for food and chemicals.

But these are small steps compared to the dream of "farming" vast quantities of food from acreage on the bottom of the sea. Tremendous problems exist. It is physically difficult to get to the bottom. New techniques will have to be worked out to solve many aspects of sowing, maintenance, and harvesting. Further, some of the abundant foods spoken of by many who favor sea farming are not very good in taste. Plankton, the broth that is found extensively in the seas, has varieties that would probably be very poorly received by most people.

Oceanographers caution those who speak of the tremendous storehouse of the sea to avoid expecting too much too soon. The sea is going to be farmed when it is economically necessary to do so, when man must turn to such practices to survive. Right now the pressure is not great enough, and the need clearly not vital.

Will we some day harvest a sea crop this way?

Barge

The Harvest

Harvesting Machine

The Crops

Sea Bottom

Comparison of the United States' land area with other countries provides some surprises.

Is the United States the biggest country in the world?

The United States is by no means the biggest. It is not the largest in area, it is not first in population, it does not have the longest river, or the highest mountain. There are no absolutes that can be credited to the United States in these respects.

In size the United States, with its 3,675,333 square miles, ranks fourth, preceded by Russia with 8,599,300 square miles, Canada with 3,851,809, and China with 3,691,500.

The population of the United States numbers 190,700,000 persons, but China with its 710,000,000, India with its 467,700,000, and the U.S.S.R. with its 227,000,000 outrank the United States. Even the Mississippi-Missouri-Red Rock river system with its 3,860-mile length is exceeded by the 4,132 miles of the Nile, and Mt. Everest in Nepal rises almost 9,000 feet more than Mt. McKinley.

The story is different when one looks at the nature of the physical facts taken together. The United States is located on one of the choicest combinations of climate, fertility, resources, dimensions, accessibility and scope ever made available to man. And it is worthy of note that this one country occupies an area roughly the same as that of the continent from which most of its people or their ancestors came—Europe. The area of Europe is 3,825,000 square miles, and it consists of twenty-seven different nations.

Why aren't we all swept off the earth as it spins through space so fast?

In spite of the great speed of the earth as it spins on its axis, the force of gravity firmly controls the men and objects "riding" on our planet. Gravity is the mutual attraction of all matter, and a large mass, such as a planet, pulls all objects on or near its surface toward its center.

The earth spins on its axis at a speed of about 1,000 miles per hour at the equator. An object such as a space ship, however, must accelerate to about 25,000 miles per hour to overcome the force of gravity and proceed into space. This is called "escape velocity."

At the same time that the earth is spinning on its axis at 1,000 miles per hour, it is moving in its orbit around the sun at about 66,700 miles per hour. This speed, too, creates no danger. Like all other objects in the solar system, the earth is being held in its path by the gravitational pull of the sun.

What is the invisible force that turns the wind, a plane, or a bullet racing north or south?

An object proceeding over the surface of the earth has, in addition to its own speed, the speed of the rotation of the earth, which is 1,000 miles per hour at the equator.

When a loaded gun, pointed straight east or west at the equator, is fired, the bullet shoots out with its own speed and runs its course straight and true. (A visitor from space would say that the bullet fired eastward was going 1,000 miles per hour faster than the one fired westward since the rotation of the earth is eastward. But the path would be substantially true.)

If the gun is pointed north or south, however, a different set of circumstances are observed. The bullet leaves the gun with its own speed and with the 1,000 miles per hour west-east speed given by the earth's spinning. As it races north it turns slightly to the right, or to the left if it goes south. The bullet is forced closer to the axis of rotation of the earth as it proceeds, as the Coriolis force goes into effect. This is similar to what happens to an ice skater who spins with her arms outstretched and then suddenly pulls her arms in alongside her body. Her arms must do something with the great speed they had when farther out from their axis of rotation—her body. They will race ahead and cause her to speed up. The bullet is free, not attached to any object, and it will curve in the direction of the earth's spin.

The Coriolis force causes deflection to the right of the direction in the Northern Hemisphere, to the left in the Southern Hemisphere (*left*). Since the radius of the earth is less at points north and south of the equator, the speed of the earth's rotation will cause an object moving from A to B to veer slightly from its course (*right*).

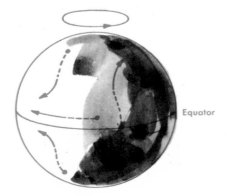

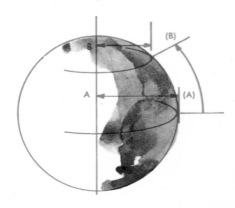

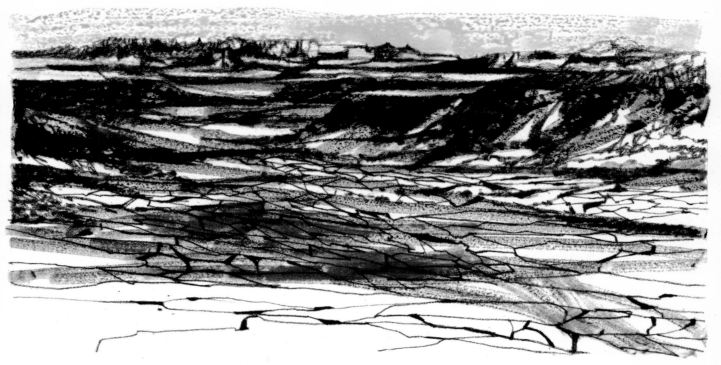

Dry Wyoming country backs up a great mountain range.

What is a Chinook?

After air is forced up and over a range of mountains and its moisture condensed from it, this now drier air is free to fall down the lee side of the range. In areas of Colorado, Wyoming, Montana, Oregon, and Washington in the western United States, the lee (in this case, the eastern) side of the mountains will experience a vast drying effect from the downsweep of dehydrated air. As the air falls thousands of feet, it becomes heated by the surroundings at lower altitudes and it moves as a moisture-absorbing wind, drying vegetation and soil in its path. The Indians gave this wind its name, Chinook.

There are sections of Wyoming which, because of this wind, are suggestive of how a science-fiction planet might appear: tremendous tables of rocky terrain baking in relentless sun; mountains eroded to weird shapes by time, temperature, and rain, looming in the distance. Some of these sections dried by the Chinooks must have been frightening to the pioneer who set out to traverse them in a wagon train with limited supplies of food and water, not knowing their extent.

Could Atlantis look like this?

Did a continent called Atlantis fall into the sea ages ago?

The legend of Atlantis goes back at least as far as the ancient Greeks. Plato wrote about a continent called "Atlantis" west of the "Pillars of Hercules," the Gibraltar strait, that had disappeared nine thousand years before. The continent was said to have been populated by an advanced civilization rich in accomplishments.

Modern man has attempted to track down this story. Whether or not Plato really meant what he wrote, many have attached great significance to the idea of a lost continent. Frequently they will point to other early references to "lost people" as being evidence. They will see connections in the finding of submerged rocks in the Atlantic Ocean, they will indicate the area around the Azores as being good prospecting ground in a search of the Atlantis remains. Every new sounding of the depths will be evaluated for its Atlantis possibilities.

Atlantis' disappearance into the sea would have been eleven thousand years ago. It is an interesting coincidence that places the event at about the time of the retreat of the last Ice Age. The intriguing part of the story comes when one imagines a glorious civilization flooded by the rising of the seas as the glaciers melted and raised the water level.

Unfortunately no real evidence has yet been found to prove this exciting tale that a once civilized continent slipped below the surface of the Atlantic. As is true with many theories, wishful thinking on the part of the believers probably has more to do with keeping the idea alive than fact has.

Where in the world was the land of Mu?

This is the Pacific version of the lost continent legend. Long ago, the tales relate, the land of Mu basked in the splendor of the Pacific sun, and then was covered by the sea: Attempts have been made without avail to track the disappearance of this land.

In his adventures at Easter Island in the central south Pacific, described in his book *Aku Aku,* Thor Heyerdahl tells of paved roads that go down to the shore and into the sea. They seem to penetrate deep into the water. Over the years legend had had it that Easter Island was the remains of Mu, and that these roads led along the sea bottom to the sunken continent, buried in the water.

Heyerdahl, a scientist, sent a scuba diver down into the water to try to trace the roads along the sea bottom. But the roads stopped after only a few feet in the water, and the land of Mu was not to be found. A little sleuthing led to the conclusion that the roads were used long ago as landing ramps for native cargo craft.

Why are great cities
usually not located at the mouths of rivers?

Rivers are very shifty things. Through the course of time they will change direction and path according to flood, drought, and changes in the level of the surface of the earth. Over the centuries huge delta systems will develop with the deposit of silt carried down to the sea by rivers. The great Mississippi, for example, lays down silt which extends the land two hundred additional feet into the Gulf of Mexico every year.

New Orleans, the large and prosperous Gulf port city on the Mississippi River, is a vital gateway for shipping in the South. It would be vulnerable to the river's whims if it were not connected by relatively open water to the east directly to the Gulf.

The Hwang Ho, or Yellow River, of China drained directly into the Yellow Sea until about one hundred years ago. A tremendous flood altered its course, making it enter the Gulf of Chihli 250 miles north! A city that had depended upon the Yellow River for commercial traffic would have died with that event.

Why is grass so important?

There are many reasons, but one is enough to express its value beyond argument. It holds the soil in place. Vast tracts of grassland in many areas of the world keep the soil from being washed away in heavy rain and blown away in drought. Regardless of how nice it looks as a lawn, or how much wild life feeds on it, the fact remains that a great deal of the surface of the earth would be mud and dust if it weren't protected by grasslands. Grass is so important that some of the great grasslands of the world have been given special names. In the United States we have named them prairies, in Russia they are known as the steppe. The gauchos of Argentina call their grassland the pampas.

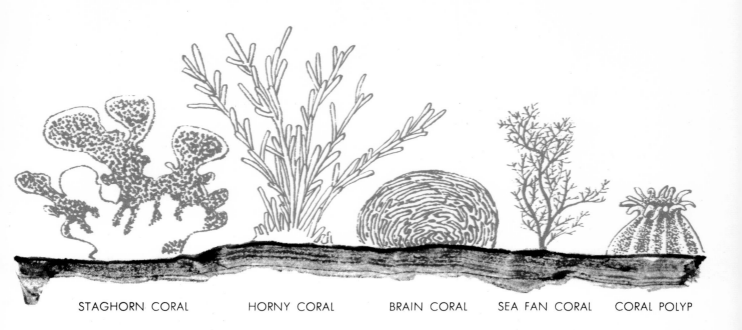

STAGHORN CORAL   HORNY CORAL   BRAIN CORAL   SEA FAN CORAL   CORAL POLYP

Where in the world
do people live on vast piles of skeletons?

This happens in Bermuda, on the atolls of the South Pacific—wherever there are coral islands.

Coral is a simple animal living on the sea bottom in a great variety of forms. Stony, sea pen, staghorn, sea fan, precious, leaf, brain, and star are just a few of the names. The coral uses lime from the sea water to build its form and a protective housing or skeleton. The "house" is left behind as new coral forms in a long cycle of life. Over thousands of years these discarded skeletons have built up such massive dimensions that islands have been formed.

Bermuda is coral; many islands in the Pacific are bordered by coral atolls that have formed around volcanic prominences. The Great Barrier Reef off northeast Australia is an immense coral formation. In many parts of the world people live on the "skeletons" of billions of tiny creatures of the sea.

83

Is it true that we are safely out of the Ice Ages?

Scientists generally agree that the retreat of the great glaciers which extended as far south as Wisconsin only eleven thousand years ago is still going on. Observations indicate glaciers are apparently still in a state of melting and reduction. If there is a regular cycle of advance and retreat that can be expected to continue, the onset of the next Ice Age could be many thousands of years from now.

Shorter-term cycles of climate change do occur, however, that can upset man's schemes. The Norsemen explored and colonized Greenland in the tenth century, but permanent settlement was discouraged afterward by a distinct and lasting change in climate that made the area unsuitable for further colonization.

Where is the great "iceberg factory"?

Greenland is a huge island ringed by mountains, and it is covered by an ice cap thousands of feet thick. Through passes in the mountains flow glaciers that are pushed to the sea by the immense pressures of the frigid mass inland. When the glaciers reach the sea, gigantic ice sheets break off along the edges in chunks that join the ocean currents. The chunks, or icebergs, float away in the Labrador Current southward to meet the Gulf Stream coming from the southwest. Then they travel northeast with the Gulf Stream until they finally melt. More icebergs are produced from the Greenland glaciers than from any other place.

A gigantic berg is different from pack ice. The berg is a *fresh-water* mass of ice originating from such glaciers as the Greenland ice cap in the north and from the glacier cap over the Antarctic continent in the south. Pack ice is frozen *sea water*, generally not as thick and massive, originating in the regions of the polar ends of the earth subject to prolonged freezing.

How far can an iceberg travel before it melts?

There have been reports of icebergs sighted only 2,000 miles north of the equator in the North Atlantic and only 1,700 miles south of the equator in the South Atlantic. These sightings prove that icebergs can travel far into the temperate zone, almost into the tropics, before they finally melt.

Impressive enough to dispel thoughts that icebergs are just chunks of rapidly melting ice is the story of the *Titanic*. In 1912 the magnificent liner, on her maiden voyage from Liverpool, England, to New York, struck a berg and went to the bottom with a loss of 1,517 lives. Some days after, a ship sighted a huge iceberg in the area. The iceberg was marked as if a ship had struck it and rubbed along its side, most of which is under water. The berg finally melted, of course, but this mass of temporarily frozen water, if it was the one responsible, was a menace long enough to tear a hole in a great ocean liner.

Icebergs can travel far enough to be a danger to ships. After the *Titanic* tragedy a North Atlantic ice patrol was organized, using American vessels financed jointly by the nations whose ships used the sea lanes afflicted by the iceberg hazard. The patrol warns of iceberg danger and keeps ships away from the dangerous lanes during the iceberg season.

Icebergs are treacherous. Only about an eighth of their mass shows above the surface of the sea.

Do all of the oceans
have the same amount of salt?

The salt content of oceans and seas is influenced by their depth and the currents, and by rivers which empty into them. Melting ice and conditions of enclosure also affect the saltiness of waters. The world-wide average for saltiness is 35 parts per 1,000. The waters of the North Atlantic and Pacific are nearly 33 in some areas. The Mediterranean Sea, because it is largely blocked except for the Strait of Gibraltar, has about 39 parts per 1,000, the Red Sea about 40. The cold waters of the Gulf of Bothnia, which lies between Finland and Sweden, has a salt content approaching zero.

Have the oceans
always been the same depth?

Even ignoring the long period of time required to fill the seas with water, we still cannot say their depth has been constant.

Two major factors have apparently had much to do with a variable sea level. One is the locking of moisture in the ice caps. Our planet has seen several major ice ages during which more than the polar regions have been covered with ice sheets thousands of feet thick. Fanning out to blanket large portions of Europe, Asia, and North America, these ice sheets locked up so much water that the level of the seas was lowered by as much as three hundred feet. This has probably happened several times. There is evidence along the present shores that ancient shore lines were much farther out than they are now. Paralleling most land areas of the earth today are plateaus under the sea. These may be the remnants of ancient beaches. If the ice presently locked in the polar caps were to melt, the level of the seas would rise farther, perhaps as much as six hundred additional feet.

This is not a clear-cut picture, however. A second factor must be considered. The surface of the earth—exposed land and sea bottom alike —is known to be subject to an eternal restlessness. Over millions of years some areas will rise, others fall, at incredibly slow, but nonetheless important, rates. This results in a change in the shape and depth of the basins that hold water. The weight of the gigantic ice caps also press down on the earth to lower land levels. Where the ice cap has retreated, even to this day the land is rising. Scandinavia's rise is at the rate of about four-tenths of an inch per year.

What would you see looking back at earth from space, 4,500 miles over the island of Tahiti?

You would see water everywhere. New Zealand would be the only major land area visible. A careful examination would reveal the islands of Polynesia, but they are very small. This area is almost all water. As a matter of fact water is dominant on the entire surface of our planet.

To use the word "earth" as our planet's name, and at the same time use the same word for soil, is really an error. Our planet should be more nautically named. The Pacific Ocean from east to west stretches more than halfway around the world, and 73 per cent of the earth's surface is covered with water. Viewed from far out in space, our sphere must be a blinding image with all of that reflected sunlight from the water surface. If the earth were smooth, with no mountains or valleys or ocean canyons, it would be covered with water to a depth of 12,000 feet. We live on the relatively small area not covered by the seas.

Where did all the water come from?

The oceans have been filling with water for perhaps one or two billion of the earth's five billion years. Theories that the oceans were formed in a fantastic deluge that brimmed the basins in a matter of a few thousand years are now shelved. Many scientists believe that hundreds of thousands of years were required to do most of the job, that a combination of steady rainfall and direct filling from the crust of the earth is responsible, and that water is still being added.

The source of all of this moisture is the interior of the earth. Volcanoes on land add gases to the atmosphere that fall as rain; volcanoes and fissures in the sea bottom add chemicals and water directly into the seas as "juvenile" water. Perhaps one-fifth of the present water content of the seas came originally from a great rain. After that, volcanoes added to this directly, and rain continued to play its part. But as much as a billion years ago, the oceans were almost full. They have been added to since, slowly but steadily.

Why are the seas so salty?

The rainfall that partially filled the original ocean basins, and that has continued to wash over the surface of the earth in an unending cycle, is a dissolving agent, the most powerful general dissolving agent of all liquids. This rainfall has acted upon the rocks that form the crust of the earth, and has washed into the sea the minerals of which these rocks are composed. Salt is one of these minerals. It remains in solution; it does not settle and separate. Volcanoes under the sea also force many chemicals, including salt, into the ocean water. This adds to its chemical content. The accumulation that has been going on for such a long period of time has resulted in the saltiness of the sea today.

Why aren't most lakes salty?

Lakes are young compared to oceans. Many lakes are the result of Ice Age glaciers that scooped out basins in the land and left them filled with melted water. Geologists believe the Great Lakes were valleys that were further excavated, filled, and dammed up by glaciers. As recently as eleven or twelve thousand years ago there were ice sheets in Wisconsin. In terms of the accumulation of salts, this is so recent that it is only the beginning of the time required to match the salt content of the oceans.

Of equal importance is the fact that a good balance of flow in and out of a lake will keep the mineral concentration at about the same level as the stream and river sources. These sources and the lake do have salt, but it never increases very much in concentration.

The Great Salt Lake and the Caspian Sea (really a lake) are examples of lakes that do not have adequate in-and-out balance of water, and have become increasingly concentrated with salt. The one big outlet that such salt lakes have is by evaporation, and that process takes water away, but not salt.

On a large scale, therefore, lakes are not particularly salty when they have a flow of water out of the basin. When they become stopped up, they cease to have "fresh" water.

The melting ice of a glacier feeds a beautiful fresh-water lake high in the mountains.

What is the difference between an ocean and a sea?

Popular usage has confused this pretty much. Rivers go "down to sea," men "to sea" in ships, we sail over the "ocean blue" and over the "ocean depths." If you want to be technical about it, though, an ocean is a major body of water, while a sea is a region in or adjoining one of the oceans. The region can be out in the open with rather indefinite borders, such as the Caribbean Sea, the Barents Sea, and the Philippine Sea, or strictly defined, such as the Red Sea and the Black Sea.

Is the water in all the oceans cold?

The waters at the surface range in temperature from near freezing to as high as 90 degrees F., all depending upon where you are and at what time of the year.

If you go down far enough, though, a steady drop in temperature will be experienced anywhere in the seas. The bottom water in the oceans is fed by a generally constant flow from the Arctic and Antarctic regions, and at depths of approximately 10,000 feet the thermometer will be near freezing most everywhere.

Even at the equator, the temperature in the Pacific Ocean is approximately 33 degrees F. at roughly 13,000 feet deep.

Does the water in the oceans move only in waves?

The water really doesn't move in waves as much as appearances indicate. But it does do a great deal of moving in the form of currents and tides. Currents have been called "rivers in the sea," that have a tremen-

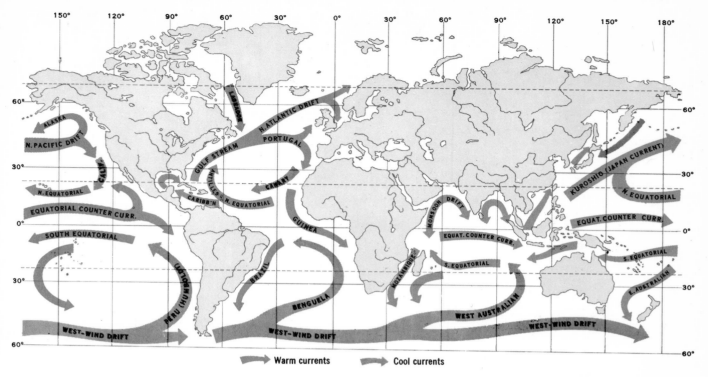

Map labels: 150° 120° 90° 60° 30° 0° 30° 60° 90° 120° 150° 180°

60° 60°

ALASKA
N. PACIFIC DRIFT
30° CALIF. 30°
N. EQUATORIAL
EQUATORIAL COUNTER CURR.
0° SOUTH EQUATORIAL
LABRADOR
N. ATLANTIC DRIFT
PORTUGAL
GULF STREAM
ANTILLES N. EQUATORIAL
CARIBB'N
CANARY
GUINEA
KUROSHIO (JAPAN CURRENT)
N. EQUATORIAL
EQUAT. COUNTER CURR.
S. EQUATORIAL
BRAZIL
PERU (HUMBOLDT)
BENGUELA
MOZAMBIQUE
MONSOON DRIFT
EQUAT. COUNTER CURR.
S. EQUATORIAL
WEST AUSTRALIAN
E. AUSTRALIAN
30° 30°
WEST-WIND DRIFT   WEST-WIND DRIFT   WEST-WIND DRIFT
60° 60°

→ Warm currents   → Cool currents

The ocean currents of the world.

dous influence upon the lands of the world. These currents are for many people a blessing from the sea that brings a climate to their part of the earth that they otherwise might not have. There are cold water and warm water currents. Europe enjoys a climate warmer than its distance north of the equator would indicate. Currents offshore bring a steady flow of warm water in the form of the Gulf Stream, which carries equatorial water in a great clockwise sweep from the West Indies north, northeast, and east to bathe the European shore and air.

Would someone living on the Persian Gulf go to the beach for a cooling dip in the summer?

He might enjoy getting wet, but it would be more like a hot bath than a swim. The Persian Gulf is in a sun-baked area of the world, and it is a long, exposed inlet from the Arabian Sea. In the summer, water temperatures of 90 degrees F. are common.

Is the ocean bottom smooth?

It was once thought to be largely level stretches of smooth muddy bottom. Oceanography, the study of the oceans, has shown that this is not the case. There are considerable areas that are covered with silt washed into the water from the land, and there are huge shelves adjacent to the land, the continental shelves, that are relatively smooth. But the ocean bottom is interrupted by mountains, volcanoes, ridges, cliffs, and canyons.

The more that oceanographers chart the ocean bottom, the more they discover of the irregularity of the vast areas hidden by the water. Before the invention of modern electronic methods, the depth of water in any spot was determined by dropping a line over the side of a ship. Hours might be required to make one measurement of depth. Charts revealed only what amounted to spot checks, and only the information from many years of work gave any real idea of the contours below.

Oceanographers have likened the process of dealing directly with the bottom of the sea to flying at ten thousand feet, dropping a line through dense clouds to the ground below, and trying to figure out what the surface looks like, how far down it is, and who lives there. We probably know more of the contours of the surface of the moon than we do of our earth's pattern under the seas.

What salt sea is
really the largest lake in the world?

The Caspian Sea, shared by the U.S.S.R. and Iran, is the largest land-locked body of water on the earth. It is a salt lake, 152,084 square miles in area, comprising the lowest depression on the European continent, 92 feet below sea level. By comparison, Lake Superior, which is the largest fresh water lake, is 31,820 square miles in area.

Were you surprised that the Caspian Sea is a part of the European continent? It is true. And the Dead Sea, which is about 700 miles *west* of the Caspian Sea, is the lowest depression in *Asia* and in the world.

Is the greatest ocean depth equal to the height of the tallest mountain?

Once it was commonly held that the high mountains of the world would neatly fill the chasms and valleys of the ocean floor. But an imaginary move of the world's highest mountain, Everest, proves the greater depth of the ocean. If Mt. Everest were dropped into the deepest part of the Marianas Trench (36,198 feet) or even into the Challenger Deep (35,-800 feet), its 29,028-foot summit would be covered by more than a mile of the ocean's water.

Can you imagine Everest at the bottom of the sea?

What is a wave?

A wave is really a rotating motion of water. If you could get down in the water and peek at the action of the water in a wave, you would see that the surface of the water is changing according to the shape of the wave as it moves, while the particles of water are rotated around and around in response to this.

The motion of a wave as it breaks at shore comes from the fact that the sea bottom interrupts the rotary motion and collapses the wave. Surfboard riders are not really being driven into shore by moving water; they are going "downhill" on the part of a wave that slants toward shore. The next time you see someone in real life, or in the movies, surf riding, notice that he is actually coasting down a hill of water that happens to be moving into shore.

The rotation of the water in a wave makes a floating bottle move back and forth like a pendulum. If there is no wind, or no current, the bottle will not travel along the surface of the sea.

WAVE MOVEMENT ⟶

A surf rider goes "downhill" on a wave profile. Away from shore, water particles rotate from the top of the water toward the bottom of the sea. As a wave approaches the shore the sea bottom interferes with the rotation of the water particles and the wave "breaks."

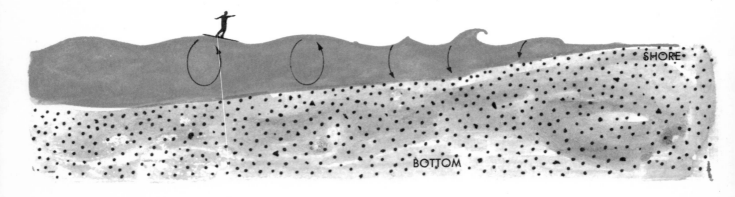

SHORE

BOTTOM

Another terror born of earthquakes.

What is a tidal wave?

It is a great wave from the sea, usually the result of an earthquake, and it can be one of the most destructive forces that the sea brings to bear against man. A tidal wave has no connection with the ordinary ebb and flow of the oceans, and the "tidal" portion of its name is a misnomer. Started by underseas earthquakes or volcanoes, tidal waves have been known to travel thousands of miles at 450 miles per hour and to cause a rise of as much as 100 feet in water level on shore. The Japanese call them *tsunamis,* and many lives have been lost to them in Japan. One in 1896 killed more than 27,000 persons.

How do men meet the danger of tidal waves?

A system of warning has been developed in recent years to give people time to get to high ground before the assault of tidal waves gets to their shore. The United States Coast and Geodetic Survey has established a network of reporting stations that co-operate to analyze potential disaster. Earthquakes reported as having occurred underseas are plotted to calculate their intensity and the possible effect of tidal waves from them; the distance to various shores is figured and the approximate time for a wave to reach these points. Warnings are then flashed by radio and cable to these points so the people can get to safe ground. The 1964 Alaska earthquake caused a tidal wave to slam into Hawaii. Warning of its approach prevented any loss of life in the fiftieth state.

95

Is there water under the ground?

There is a natural supply of water found in the ground, put there by rain, snow, and melted ice. For untold centuries springs and wells have been tapped for basic water needs. The oasis of the desert owes its being to the supply of water in the ground. But man's use of this supply is sometimes at a rate greater than its replacement by normal means. Except for great changes in climate, there is no way to substantially increase the hidden supply.

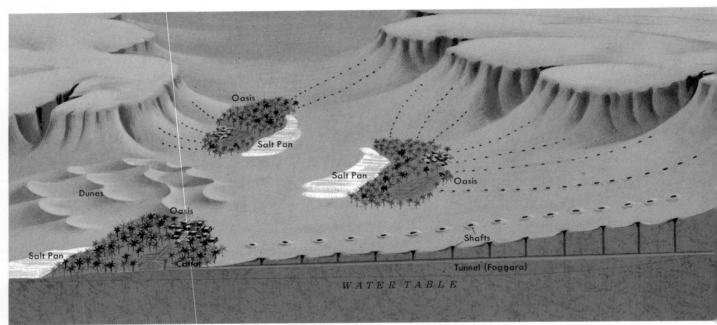

A water table under the desert is tapped by a "foggara," a man-made tunnel which draws off the water into the canals of the oases. Shafts let men get down to the tunnel.

What is the water table?

The level of water in the ground, a kind of underground sea, is called a water table. Roughly parallel to the surface, and anywhere from a few inches to hundreds of feet below, water will collect in the pores of rock or various kinds of subsoil and form a reservoir that can be tapped.

If the table is near the surface, a large shaft can be sunk down to the water and the bottom of the shaft will be flooded. The old-fashioned well is of this type, and there are still many around the world. When a large supply of water is needed, a pipe can be driven down and the water pumped up to spigots or to an organized water supply.

When the natural supply of water is being used too rapidly, the condition is referred to as a drop in the water table. If the water is used at a rate greater than natural supply can balance, the table drops farther down into the ground. It becomes harder to pump the water up to the surface, and the water table may even disappear because of differing subterranean structure. It is common to have to drill several hundred feet through clay and limestone to find adequate flows of water for wells. Thousands of communities depend entirely on wells for all of their water, and they are, in many cases, finding it increasingly difficult to get enough of the precious liquid.

What is an artesian well?

This is an example of long-distance pumping action given free by nature. Rain and melting snow seep into the ground through exposed rock formations which connect directly to rock underlying some distant point. If the distant point, which may be hundreds of miles away, is lower than the source, water flowing through the pores and cracks in the rock will have a "head." That is, it will have pressure from gravity. Someone tapping that subterranean flow of water will find it gushing upward into his waiting hands, or pail.

The water is simply obeying the natural law that water seeks its own level. Here, the water wants to get back up to the level at which it started. The artesian-well opening is its outlet.

In the following pairs of locations, which is farther north?

a. *New York and Madrid*
b. *Seattle and Berlin*
c. *Los Angeles and Rome*
d. *Venice and Vladivostock*
e. *London and Newfoundland*
f. *Chicago and Barcelona*

Take out a world map, or check your globe. By comparing the latitudes of the pairs of locations above, you will find the following answers:

a. The latitude of New York and Madrid is virtually identical, but New York (40.40 degrees N.) is a little farther north than Madrid (40.26 degrees N.).

b. Berlin is about 400 miles north of Seattle.

c. Rome is about 600 miles north of Los Angeles.

d. Venice and Vladivostok lie at almost identical latitudes, but Venice (45.25 degrees N.) is a little farther north than Vladivostok (43.06 degrees N.).

e. London is north of Newfoundland.

f. Chicago and Barcelona also have virtually identical north-south locations, but Chicago (41.49 degrees N.) is a little farther north than Barcelona (41.25 degrees N.).

What and where in the world is Taumatawhaka-tangihangakoauauatamateapokaiwhenuakitananatahu?

This is a village in the southern Hawke Bay district of North Island, New Zealand. In the Maori language this long name means "the brow of the hill where Tametea, the man with the big knee who slid, climbed and swallowed mountains, the discoverer of land, played his flute to his loved one."

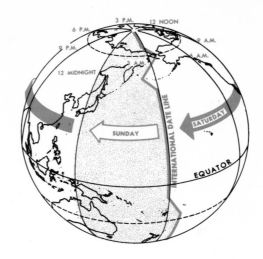

Men have agreed to respect an imaginary line on the earth to help separate one day from another.

Where in the world can today become yesterday?

Earth is a nearly spherical body in space, making a full turn on its axis once in every twenty-four hours. It always exposes half its surface to sunlight, while the other half is unlighted by the sun. These periods of light and nonlight we call night and day. Men have devised a time system for marking each revolution of earth, calling it a calendar day. To change from one day to another he has arbitrarily chosen midnight, 12:00 P.M., or 2400 hours, that point which is approximately in the middle of the period between sunset and sunrise.

Of course, it cannot be midnight all over the world at the same time for we are imposing the concept of time on a physical, constantly changing condition. As the earth spins from west to east on its axis, "midnight" moves with it, toward the west. The change from one day to the next is happening some place in the world all the time. So, there had to be some *man-made* north-south line on earth along which the *calendar day* ends and a new one starts. Men have agreed that the 180th meridian will be this changing point, and they named it the International Dateline. It passes through an area of the mid-Pacific where there is very little land. Its location prevents its troubling large concentrations of population.

When you cross the International Dateline going west, *today* becomes *tomorrow;* when you cross the International Dateline going east, *today* becomes *yesterday.*

Is a seamount animal, vegetable, or mineral?

It is mineral and cannot be seen unless you are in a bathyscaphe. Seamounts are undersea volcanic cones dotting the floors of the Atlantic and Pacific in countless numbers. Because of their apparent widespread distribution, most seamounts probably have not even been located yet. The cone of a seamount, the result of ancient volcanic activity, may rise thousands of feet from the sea bottom.

During World War II, H. H. Hess, a geologist from Princeton University who was on duty as the commanding officer of a Navy transport, used his ship's echo sounder (an instrument that continuously records a profile of the ocean bottom on a graph) in the discovery of a particular kind of seamount in the Pacific. He discovered a number of volcanic cones that had flat tops. He called these "guyots" (pronounced *ghee'o*). Since his first discoveries, hundreds of guyots have been located. Oceanographic expeditions have dredged beach gravels and fossils from the flat tops of some of them.

It is as if this particular type of seamount had been islands which were mysteriously dropped down into the sea. A guyot may rise as much as 15,000 feet high, and its top still be 1,500 feet below the surface of the water. Scientists think that perhaps over a period of as much as twenty million years the bottom level and the water volume of the ocean changed enough to bury volcanic islands. The sea water protected the ancient forms and kept the guyots intact for men to examine.

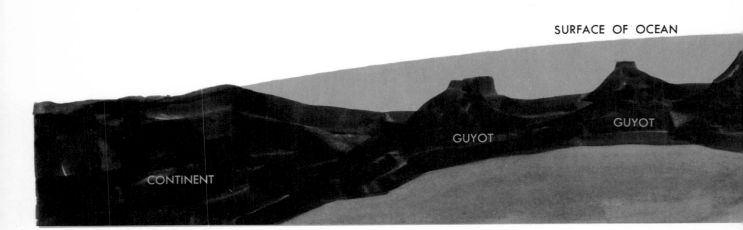

SURFACE OF OCEAN

GUYOT

GUYOT

CONTINENT

What is the Sargasso Sea?

About eight hundred miles southeast of New York is Bermuda, a British island possession in the Atlantic. It is located in the center of what is called the Sargasso Sea. For centuries this sea was described in sailor lore as a mass of seaweed so thick that ships unlucky enough to enter it were held fast and could not escape. Authors wrote strange stories based on these tales—stories which described entire colonies of ships stuck fast in the weeds, their helpless passengers forced to live out their lives in the floating field. Bermuda residents don't take this fiction very seriously, nor do the crews of the many ships which regularly cruise the waters of the Sargasso Sea without any trouble at all.

Actually, the Sargasso Sea is an inner oval of ocean water enclosed by the currents of the Gulf Stream, the Portugal Current, the Canary Current, and the North Equatorial Drift. These currents flow around the Sargasso Sea in a clock-wise direction. Because of these currents, the level of the water in the center of the oval is about two feet higher than at the edges. In spite of sailor lore, the waters of this shoreless sea, hundreds of thousands of square miles in area, are among the clearest and deepest blue of all ocean waters. Sargassum weed which gives the sea its name grows in patches that float in bands sometimes stretching as far as the eye can see. Fish peculiar to the weed bunches swim in the waters. But there is no vast, thick jungle of seaweed which makes the Sargasso Sea a hazard to ships.

Some undersea mountains have peaks, others are flat on top.

UNT   SEA MOUNTS   GUYOTS   ISLAND

Which is bigger,
the Sahara Desert or the United States?

The Sahara covers approximately 3,000,000 square miles, the United States 3,600,000. The desert is about one-quarter of all of the African continent in area, and it is one of the most forbidding parts of the world.

Is the Sahara Desert one vast stretch of sand dunes
with blistering temperatures?

Contrary to popular concepts, deserts are not all dunes with Foreign Legionnaires always coming over the next crest. Sand comes from cracked and eroded wind-blown rock, and some source must be nearby for the sand to exist. The Sahara has its share of lovely dunes, but large parts of this wasteland are mountains, rocks, gullies, ageless stone prominences, and dry river beds. Some of the elevations in the Sahara Desert approach or exceed 10,000 feet. Two of these high points are mountains in Chad—Pic Tousidé (10,712 feet) and Emi Koussi (11,204 feet). Mt. Tahat in Algeria rises 9,852 feet.

Desert landscape can vary.

The desert is hot. The highest official temperature ever recorded on earth was registered in Libya, 136.4 degrees F. in 1922. But the desert is not always blistering hot. In some of its towns these low temperatures have been recorded: 22 degrees F. at El Golea, Algeria; 25 degrees F. at In-Salah, Algeria; and 28 degrees F. at Wadi Halfa, Sudan.

Where is the Gobi Desert?

On the high plateau of Mongolia, the home of Genghis Khan's ancestors, is an area that is the easternmost extension of a desert belt that extends from the west coast of Africa. This is the Gobi Desert. It's the end of a series of dry, desert lands that spread from Africa through the Sahara into Arabia and on across Iraq and Iran into Russia, over western China, and into Outer Mongolia.

Compared to the Arabian desert, authorities say that the Gobi is misnamed as desert land. In Mongolia the word *gobi* refers to a stretch of low-lying land, arid because it is low-lying, and with sparse vegetation. There is a table of water which flows beneath the surface of the *gobi,* and livestock are watered from wells dug in the region. The terrain of the Gobi Desert is far less forbidding than the hot, sand-swept deserts of the Middle East.

How close to the center of the earth has man gone?

The world's deepest mine, the Kalar Gold Field, Mysore State, India, reaches 9,811 feet into the earth. Yet a man working on the lowest level of this mine would not be as close to the center of the earth as man can come. Due to the flattening of the earth's shape at the poles, an explorer at the North Pole, simply standing on the ice there, would be thirteen miles closer to the center of the earth than someone standing at the equator line. The Kalar Gold Mine doesn't go down into the earth even a full two miles!

Are all rocks hard?

Most rocks are made up of grains of minerals, and the minerals vary from chalks soft enough to write on a school blackboard to diamonds hard enough to drill through steel. Furthermore, mineral rocks do not have to be different in chemical content to vary in hardness. Graphite and diamond are identical chemically; yet graphite, the primary ingredient of the "lead" pencil, is one of the softest mineral substances known, and diamond is one of the hardest. Graphite is opaque, while diamond is transparent. The way the raw material is put together physically makes the difference in the hardness effect.

What did the prospector prove
when he panned gold in a stream?

For one thing he proved that if the stream had particles of gold distributed all along its bed, it might be worthwhile to "mine" the stream itself and gather a tidy sum of the precious stuff.

But the basic thing the prospector was doing was gathering evidence of a gold source upstream. A gold vein that was exposed and subject to the washing effects of water would release particles of gold into the stream or river bed. But veins largely used up, or staked out by someone else, might leave evidence in the streams long after the vein was washed away. Sometimes the prospector was disappointed.

The prospector also was demonstrating the results of placer mining, a process in which water is used to wash gold out of a vein deliberately. This is called hydraulic mining, and has been used in many parts of the world.

What is in the center of the earth?

Scientists, of course, have no first-hand knowledge of anything deeper than the world's deepest wells. In the Gulf of Mexico, south of New Orleans, a 22,570-foot test bore was accomplished in 1956, but this is a mere dent compared to the almost 4,000 miles to the earth's center. However, scientists do theorize that the center of the earth is a nickel-iron core having a diameter of a little over 4,000 miles and a temperature of 4,000 to 8,000 degrees F. The theories expressed today generally state that below the immediate surface (under the "film" of soil) there is a rock crust 4 to 20 miles thick; then a mantle 1,800 miles deep; and finally an outer core 1,375 miles wide and an inner core 1,600 miles in diameter. The two cores total 2,175 miles in radius.

A diagram showing the layers of the earth.

CRUST
MANTLE
OUTER CORE
INNER CORE

4–20 miles

1,800 miles

1,375 miles

800 miles

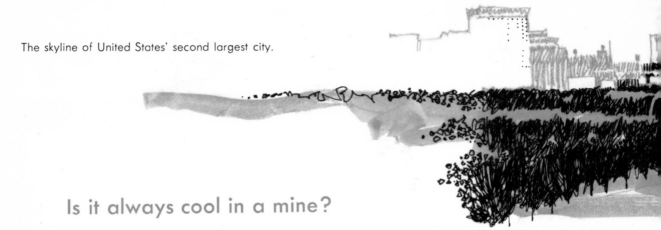

The skyline of United States' second largest city.

Is it always cool in a mine?

It is true that in even the hottest places on earth there is a stable moderate temperature only a few feet below the surface. Many wells are noted for their cool water, frequently around 55 degrees. But this is only a very local condition due to the insulating qualities of soil and rock. This insulation is overcome the deeper one goes, and there is a steady increase of temperature. The result is that deep mines are uncomfortably hot. Gold mines in the Transvaal, South Africa, as deep as 8,500 feet, will register a temperature of about 40 degrees F. *above* the average temperature at the surface.

What continent is almost hidden from sight?

The Antarctic continent is almost completely covered by a sheet of snow and ice that averages more than one mile in thickness. Larger than Australia or Europe, almost as large as South America, Antarctica is a rugged, forbidding icescape, punctured by mountains and snow-free valleys in only a few places. As recently as 1952, very little was known about the land below the ice sheet that covers the continent. We have learned only recently that the south magnetic pole under this ice sheet is moving constantly, having shifted position more than a hundred miles in the past eight or ten years—six hundred miles since just before the First World War!

106

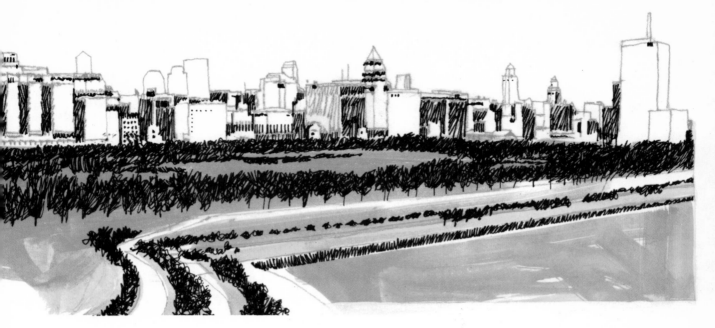

What city of the United States is built on what was once onion patches, swamps, and lake?

Its name comes from an Indian word that has been variously translated as "skunk," "wild onion," and "powerful," all of which point to one thing—Chicago was a place of pretty strong odor to the American Indians. The odor came from large patches of onion found growing wild in the area.

Located at the southwestern portion of the tip of Lake Michigan, the Chicago of today occupies about twenty-five miles of the Lake Michigan shore line, almost all of which is public park. Chicago has built most of its shore by scooping up lake bottom and depositing it, layer by layer, along the water's edge. Years ago the lake waves were where boulevards and apartment and office buildings are today.

Inland the land also has been built up to a certain degree. Through the years it has been standard practice to take the soil that is excavated to build the foundation of a house and replace it around the completed structure. This, together with a certain amount of topsoil and fill brought in from elsewhere, has gradually raised the level of many sections. Only a few miles to the southwest, the land slopes to a level that is actually below that of Lake Michigan.

Is South America all jungle?

A misconception that seems to hold on is that this great continent, with the exception of a few large coastal cities, is overgrown with tropical swamp jungle, watered by rivers full of crocodiles and piranha fish, and inhabited by head-hunting, primitive man.

South America runs in latitude from 10 degrees north of the equator to about 55 degrees south. The climate varies from hot, humid equatorial to bleak cold. Tierra del Fuego is an island at the southern tip that is famed for its proximity to Cape Horn. A more storm- and fog-ridden area would be hard to find. There are deserts in northern Chile. The Amazon River has the greatest volume of flow of any river in the world. The vast mountain range called the Andes runs almost the entire north-south length of the land and is volcanic. Aconcagua, 22,834 feet high, is the highest mountain outside the continent of Asia. The extensive Brazilian campos and Argentine pampas are superior agricultural and grazing lands which are used to produce much of the world's supply of beef. No, South America is not all jungle. The jungle, which is often called the equatorial forest, is confined to the relatively small area on either side of the equator.

Machu Picchu, an ancient Incan city in the Andes.

Glaciers look like massive rivers of snow.

Is a glacier just one huge mass of ice?

It is difficult to understand that materials as massive and seemingly solid as glaciers are really rivers in motion. The fact is that much of the landscape of the earth has been carved, planed, gouged, and transported by the movement of these ice rivers.

Glaciers are ancient accumulations of snow and ice surviving from the Ice Ages. Piled high and thick on mountains, the accumulated snow-ice pushes down into gorges and valleys, making its way slowly to warmer altitudes or the sea. As the glacier moves over the terrain, it acts as an abrasive, scraping the surface. Boulders can be found today that were transported many miles in past Ice Ages. Copper from Michigan has been found in Missouri; jasper from the Georgian Bay in Canada was moved to Ohio. The most important copper mine in Finland was discovered because copper ore was traced backward along an Ice Age flow to the source.

When and where was the highest wave
ever recorded by a ship at sea?

In February of 1933, the U.S.S. *Ramapo,* traveling from Manila to San Diego, was overtaken by winds that gradually rose from 30 knots to over 60 knots (34 to 69 miles per hour). Great waves passed the ship. The watch officer on the bridge of the Navy tanker wrote that he saw "seas astern at a level above the mainmast crow's nest and at the moment of observation the horizon was hidden from view by the waves approaching the stern."

By laying out the geometry of the situation—ship's length at 478 feet, height of crow's nest, height of bridge, angle of ship with respect to the horizon—the stern of the ship was calculated to have been 112 feet below the top of the wave. The wave at the stern of the boat was 112 feet high!

Huge waves can cause a large ship to pitch forward and backward.

Line of Sight Crow's Nest Observer 11° 50'

112 ft.

Where in the world are the hottest and coldest places?

In this case, the records have been made in areas where they would be expected. The highest temperature officially recorded is 136.4 degrees F., in the shade at Azizia, Libya, Africa, in September, 1922. The lowest temperature accepted is −126.9 degrees F., at Vostok, Antarctica, in August, 1960.

In the United States, Death Valley holds the honor of recording the highest temperature, 134 degrees F., in July, 1913. Tanana, Alaska, recorded the lowest temperature, −76 degrees F., in January, 1886.

Equally as interesting as these extremes are the geographical locations which experience the greatest range of temperature. At Yakutsk, Siberia, U.S.S.R., an annual range of 181.4 degrees F. has been recorded. At Medicine Lake, Montana, a range of 175 degrees F., from 117 degrees F. to −58 degrees F., summer to winter, over the years 1921-1956, is a matter of record.

Is the water of the Red Sea really red?

It is not, and there is no positive agreement among authorities on the origin of the sea's name. However, most marine biologists accept the explanation that the "red" refers to a tiny red-pigmented microorganism, plankton, which inhabits the sea. At certain seasons this red plankton multiplies extraordinarily and brings on a "red tide" over the surface of the Red Sea. At one time the plankton may have abounded to such a degree that the sea frequently appeared red.

This explanation is not meant to overlook the beauty of a sunrise or sunset viewed across the Red Sea from the appropriate shore. The region is one of torrid heat and desert sands, and a blistering red sun at the beginning and end of daylight will present a spectacularly rosy scene that may be another reason for the name "Red Sea."

Why is the Grand Canyon like a two-billion-year-old storybook?

Since the earliest formation of the earth's crust, layer upon layer of sediment has been deposited over many areas. On the raw, early surface of Precambrian rock, great seas and lakes have laid down material that has solidified into rock. Geologists dig into these layers to learn the history of our planet. Ancient sea beds, sandstone, fossil shells, clay, flint rock, and numerous formations, each of these layers, tell a story. Frequently, though, this story is difficult for the geologist to read. A layer will be exposed by erosion and be open to inspection. But under it will be hundreds or thousands of feet of other layers too tough and deep to cut through. Sometimes the digging will be done by nature.

Seven million years ago, a river in the land we know as western Arizona flowed across a great plain, almost at sea level. Below the river bed was a two-billion-year geological record. Then the area was subjected to a great slow lifting, producing a local dome. The river, which

we know as the Colorado, began to flow more swiftly, wearing away the layers of sediment below it, cutting a canyon faster than the rising of the dome. The surrounding land rose higher and higher above the swift, narrow river bed. The walls of the canyon widened and separated to great widths, eroded by the melting snows, rain, and sun. Eventually there were mile-high walls of geological record for the scientist to read.

Two hundred seventeen miles long, ten miles wide, and one mile deep, the stupendous Grand Canyon of the Colorado River today is a direct slice through the earth's crust dating back to Precambrian rock, back to the surface of the planet at the time it is believed the very first forms of life appeared. Up the canyon walls layers of sandstone, beaches with the ripples of waves still evident, and fossil remains can be seen. Trilobites (among the earliest of animals leaving clear fossil records), shells, corals, ferns, insects, and sponges have left traces. Seas, lakes, and land are recorded here. The Grand Canyon with all of its overpowering beauty and magnitude is a unique earth-history book—a must in anyone's travel plans.

A spectacular panorama of earth's history.

Rivers show signs that can be used to uncover the secret of their age.

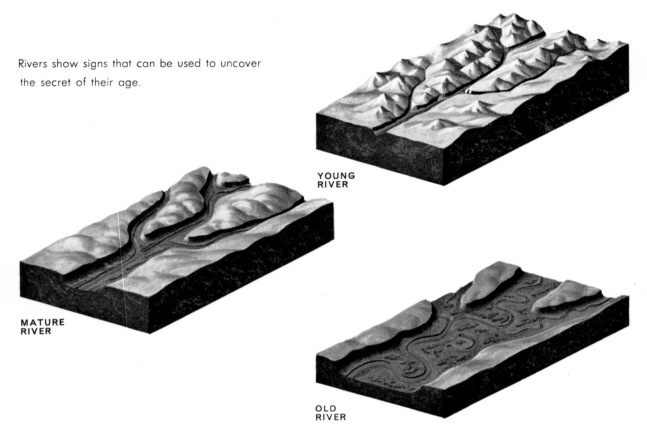

YOUNG RIVER

MATURE RIVER

OLD RIVER

Do rivers show their age?

Such rivers as the Colorado at the Grand Canyon, which exposes a seven-million-year-old canyon wall, tell their age boldly, vividly. Other rivers with shorter histories also have telltale marks. The path of the original courses, how steep the valley is, whether flooding has affected the nearby terrain, and how the river beds have altered through the years—all these will reveal age.

Typically, a young river will have a swift flow, rapids, waterfalls, and a narrow course through the land. An older river will run through a wider valley, with the valley walls a gentle slope. The aged river will meander over a wide floor, and at flood it may fill the valley. The valley floor will be built up from river sediment. Normally, the river will have a zigzag course, wandering in a variety of bends.

114

What is an ox-bow lake?

An old river will meander over many different paths of a wide bed. Following the path of least resistance, the old river may even wander in loops, rejoining itself somewhat downstream of the point where it started to loop. In the course of time, the river will short-cut from the point where it started to loop across the land to the point where the loop returns to the stream bed, thus cutting off the loop. The lake that forms in the abandoned loop-course is called an ox-bow.

Also, old bends abandoned by the river may be refilled temporarily by flood or seepage of water through the bed soil from the river and become ox-bow lakes. Such lakes are frequently undercut and destroyed later by further meandering of the river.

Many mature rivers look like gigantic snakes when viewed from the air. The Annapolis Valley in Nova Scotia is an excellent example.

Does a river make a good boundary?

A river is better than no marker, but sometimes it is unreliable. Rivers flowing in confined gorges, where actually the gorge forms the boundary, are fairly reliable. For example, the Hudson River forms a good boundary marker where the states of New Jersey and New York meet. But the Rio Grande River, which separates Mexico and the United States along its course from El Paso/Cuidad Juarez to the Gulf of Mexico, wanders and changes its course frequently. Subject to alternating drying and flooding, the Rio Grande meanders over territory where water is precious, also. Consequently, disputes over the changing boundary and water rights are frequent. Just recently, a long-standing dispute between the United States and Mexico was settled with a section of Texas land, near the city of El Paso, going to Mexico.

Where in the world is the longest river and what is its course?

The Nile River has its source in Lake Victoria, straddling the equator in the eastern section of Africa. From there it flows northward to its mouth at the Mediterranean Sea, a distance of 4,132 miles. No other river in the world is so long.

For ages, people had no idea how very long the Nile River is. Explorers had been hunting the source for hundreds and hundreds of years, since long before the birth of Christ. The Greek historian Herodotus explored the Nile southward as far as the first cataract at Aswan, in about 460 B.C. The Roman emperor Nero sent expeditions that failed to penetrate the swamps of the Sudan. In spite of all efforts, however, the source was not found until about a hundred years ago. John Speke, an English explorer, finally located it in 1862. Men finally knew the length of the longest river in the world.

Actually, the Nile is two rivers, the White Nile and the Blue Nile. The main course, and the one which is measured to give the entire river its length, is the White Nile. The second branch, which brings more than half of the water carried by the great river, is the Blue Nile.

A great African river flows 4,132 miles from its headwaters to the sea.

Lake Victoria, shared by Tanganyika, Uganda, and Kenya, is fed by the waters of the Kagera and other rivers which flow from the mountains to the west at an altitude of 6,000 feet. From the northern tip of Lake Victoria, the White Nile begins its journey, drops over Ripon Falls, flows into Lake Kyoga, over Murchison Falls, and into Lake Albert. The Nile's juncture with Lake Albert is only by chance; it flows in and out at the northeastern tip of the lake. The White Nile now begins to run out of help from tributaries. Its course through the Sudd, the great swamp of the Sudan, costs it 8 per cent of its water by evaporation. The Sobat River flows in after this vast area of hot swamplands, and just about makes up the amount of water lost in the Sudd.

At Khartoum, approximately halfway on its journey, the White Nile is joined by the Blue Nile, whose source is at Lake Tana in the mountains of Ethiopia. The Blue Nile supplies 63 per cent of the Nile water. Now begin the succession of cataracts, six in all, that punctuate the Nile's journey through the great arid heat of the Sudan and Egypt. Except for the Atbara River (between the sixth and fifth cataracts) the Nile receives no further replenishment. It flows unassisted for almost two thousand miles more, giving life to the land on its passage through Egypt to the Mediterranean.

Where would one go to find a wadi?

A wadi is a river that goes on vacation most of the time. Look at a map of the Sahara Desert and, if it is detailed, you will see lines drawn that indicate river beds that have water in them only during ample rains.

Deserts, despite their fame as parched land, do get rain, and it frequently falls in torrential cloudbursts brought on by seasonal variations in wind patterns. The floor of a desert cannot absorb such great amounts of water right away, and torrents wash into low spots and form a river, sweeping great amounts of soil, rock, and brush in its path.

The short-lived rain passes on, and the water soaks into the parched earth. Part of it evaporates from the soaked ground, and part filters down below. Some oases derive their supply of water from the accumulation of this rainfall in pockets in the ground.

The dry river beds are called wadis in the Sahara, arroyos in North America, and laagtes in South Africa. Some maps show the dry river-bed lines going into dotted or cross-hatched areas to indicate a pond or lake that is filled only at the time of the rains.

Can a river be forced to run backward?

Yes, a great American city owes its beautiful lake shore to man's engineering ability. Before the turn of the twentieth century, Chicago, located at the southern tip of Lake Michigan, dumped its refuse into the Chicago River which flowed into the lake. Eventually the city's water supply became polluted, and bright, clean sandy bathing beaches were not possible. The lower end of Lake Michigan was in danger of becoming a waste basin.

In 1900 city engineers took steps to correct this problem which shadowed the city's future growth. By damming the river with locks and forcing Lake Michigan water into the Chicago River, the flow of the river's waters was reversed. The river went in its new direction to join the Illinois River, whose natural flow is toward the Mississippi. The Illinois' waters join the Mississippi at a point north of St. Louis, and from here the flow is all the way to the Gulf of Mexico.

Do all rivers go down to the sea?

The general rule is that they do. The waters of the Nile, Mississippi, Amazon, and countless other major and minor rivers of the world do all flow into the open sea. They carry the run-off of rain and melting snow funneled from innumerable tributaries. The whole system drains according to a natural slope of the river bottom that continues all the way down to the sea.

There are interesting exceptions, however, proving how general rules are frequently inaccurate. Of the many examples that could be given, one is the River Jordan in the Biblical territory of the Middle East. It is a fresh-water artery vital to both Israel and Jordan. In fact, it is the subject of a heated dispute between the two countries over the diversion of its water for irrigation purposes. The Jordan flows in a cleft in the surface of the earth that is a part of a huge cut extending from Syria in the north to the Red Sea far south. But the River Jordan does not flow into a true sea. The Jordan empties into the Dead Sea, which is really a salt lake.

There are other reasons why rivers don't reach the sea. A glance at the map of Russian Siberia will show the Northern Dvina, the Pechora, the Ob and Irtysh, the Yenisey, and the Lena all flow from south to north beyond the Arctic Circle into the Arctic Ocean. Part of the year their waters don't get to the sea. The lower portions of these rivers are ice locked a long time after the headwaters have melted and are running. The mouth of the Yenisey is frozen for 260 days of the year.

Continental Divide

Rocky Mountains

High
Plateau

Appalachian Mountains

The land slopes down from the Continental Divide of North America.

What is the highest continent on earth?

It depends on your ground rules. If you consider the ice sheet over the Antarctic as surface, that continent wins the prize. Its mean elevation in feet is 6,000. But if you rule out snow and ice, honors must go elsewhere. The Antarctic ice sheet presses down on the land surface beneath with so much weight that the land is below sea level in substantial areas. Recent calculations indicate that the ice sheet may average from 6,600 to 8,200 feet in thickness!

For everyday, garden-variety continents, that is, those without an ice cap, Asia is the highest, at 3,000 feet mean elevation.

What is sea level?

It is the normal, average position of the surface of the oceans of the earth. From this average all measurements of height and depression are made. Even the height of a mountain far inland is given in relation to sea level.

The almost even pull of gravity over our nearly spherical earth keeps the oceans at a common level. Tides, currents, the interference of land areas, and the wind do influence sea level, however. Charts of coastal areas, to be on the safe side, give the depths of reefs, sand bars, and other hazards to ships at low tide. Also the surface of the ocean far from land may be three to six feet above or below what would be expected. But the elevation of the earth is based on the prevailing sea surface. Since the land level varies so much, the sea is a more conven-

120

Continental Shelf   Continental Slope   Sea Level   Bottom of the Sea

The Continental Shelf and the Continental Slope continue the incline toward the bottom of the sea.

ient and useful solution to the problem of expressing height and depth. It is also a logical solution because 73 per cent of the earth is covered by water. Such an immense cover deserves to be regarded as the surface of our planet.

What is the difference between continental divide, continental shelf, and continental slope?

The term *continental divide* has to do with the drainage pattern of surface water over a large area. In North America, on one side of this "divide" all rivers and lakes drain toward the Pacific; on the other side all drain toward the Arctic Ocean and the Atlantic, including the Gulf of Mexico. The North American continental divide runs from the Brooks and Richardson mountain ranges at the northern edge of Alaska and Canada through the Rocky Mountains of Canada and the United States into Mexico along the Sierra Madre Occidental.

The term *continental shelf* refers to the vast plateaus under the sea extending out from most shore lines. In some places these shelves are as much as three hundred miles wide. Along the coast of California the shelf is only twenty-five miles wide. These shelves are considered part of the continent that they surround.

The real edge of the continent lies in the water where the *continental slope* begins, that gradual decline, reaching from the edge of the continental shelf to the bottom of the sea.

In what direction does a ship travel going through the Panama Canal from the Atlantic to the Pacific?

It proceeds in a southeast direction. Yes, the Pacific Ocean is west of the Atlantic, but the entrance to the canal on the Atlantic side is at the Gatun Locks past Cristobal. From here to the exit, into the Pacific past Balboa, is almost exactly southeast. The land in this part of the world is a strip joining North and South America that does not run north and south. It runs northeast and southwest, and the cut was made as directly as possible across this area.

The Panama Canal cuts through a narrow neck of land joining North America and South America.

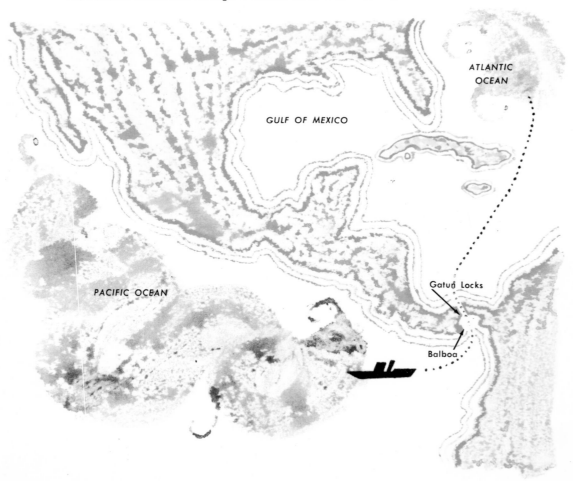

Do objects always fall straight down?

Straight down depends on where you are. Gravity varies because the earth is made up of layers of different kinds of rocks and minerals. The pull of gravity is not quite the same on top of a mountain as it is beside it. And it isn't just a matter of how high you are. Mountains are made of rock less dense than the rock under an ocean. In turn, the heavier rock layer below land and sea has a wide range of thicknesses which alter slightly the force of gravity. So, a plumb bob or a pendulum hanging "down" when you are standing on a mountain may lean a trifle because of the uneven pull under it.

But a plumb bob is not the only thing affected by differences in gravity. Athletes' records are affected by it, depending on *where* they are performing. A javelin-throw of 258 feet in Helsinki, Finland, is equal to a throw of 6 inches more in Tokyo. A broad jump of 26 feet is equal to one of an additional 1½ inches at Tokyo. This doesn't mean that there is anything unfair in the Tokyo competition. It does mean, however, that the force of gravity is greater in Helsinki than in Tokyo, and that records are not quite what they seem.

123

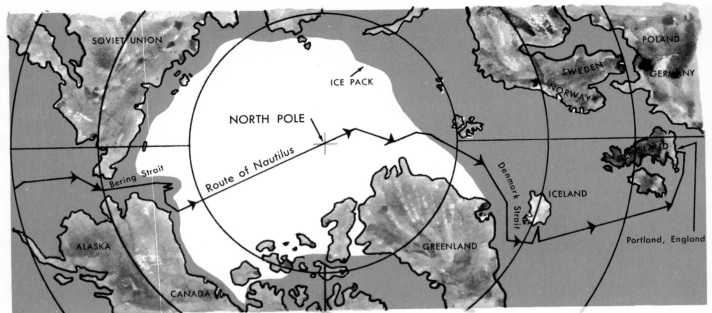

The Nautilus' 1958 route.

Has man ever set foot on the North Pole?

The North Pole has never had the staff of any nation's flag planted on its soil, nor has any man set foot on it. The North Pole is not located on Arctic land; it is rather in the midst of ice and snow in the Arctic Ocean. But it has been explored both above and below. First *to* the pole was Peary in 1909. First *under* the pole was the U.S. submarine *Nautilus,* under the command of Commander W. R. Anderson, in 1958. The atomic-powered *Nautilus* made the journey from the Pacific through the Bering Strait to the pole, and then proceeded to the Atlantic sailing east of Greenland and passing through the Denmark Strait between Greenland and Iceland.

Is there no land in the Arctic?

Although the Arctic is not a single continent, and the North Pole itself is in an ice sea, there is land in the region. Some of the land has evergreen forests with trees that grow to one hundred feet in height. Other land areas covered with moss and lichen are called tundra. Arctic sum-

124

mers bring forth grass and flowering plants, reindeer herds graze under the care of men, and fish and animal life are plentiful. The regions above the Arctic Circle (66 degrees, 30 minutes North) are shared by many nations: the U.S.S.R., the U.S.A., Canada, Denmark (Greenland), Norway, Sweden, and Finland.

Why are so many commercial aircraft flights made "over the pole"?

Studying a globe will show clearly why the shortest distance between two points on earth is a *curved line*. Earth is nearly a sphere, and the most direct route from one point to another is along a line that radiates from the center of the sphere. This line is a *great circle,* running true to the shape of the earth, rather than according to such artificial concepts as lines of direction, latitude, longitude, and zones.

By using this great circle concept, many miles can be saved in journeying by air from, say, Los Angeles to Moscow. Flying a convenience route from Los Angeles by way of New York and Paris to Moscow, mileage will be about 7,750 miles. Flying the great circle route, from Los Angeles over Canada, above the Arctic Circle close to the pole, over Greenland and down to Moscow, mileage will be about 6,070 miles. Directionally, from Los Angeles, a plane flying the great circle route will head northeast by north; by the time it is over Greenland, it will be going east; on the final leg into Moscow it will be heading southeast by south! This is a form of navigation that causes a pilot to change compass direction frequently in order to keep from turning!

The most direct route between major points will often call for crossing territory that might seem out of the way. The great circle route from Chicago to Hong Kong will cross Canada, go north of Alaska over Russia, over China west of Korea, and finally heading almost south, come down in the British Crown Colony.

Why doesn't the Po River, flowing at rooftop height through parts of Italy, flood the landscape?

The Po River originates in the French-Italian Alps in the western extreme of Italy. It flows past Turin, Italy, and proceeds all across the country to empty into the Adriatic Sea. The Po is a restless, rapidly moving river. Over many centuries it has carried vast quantities of silt toward the sea. Much of this silt has been deposited in the river bed, making the river more and more shallow as the years passed by. As far back as Roman times, people began to build levees to hold the river in its course. As the silt continued to pile up during the years, the levees have grown higher, too, so that today some of the levees are as much as thirty feet above the floor of the intensively cultivated Po Valley.

Much of the silt carried by the river has reached the Adriatic, however, and has been dropped at the mouth of the river to form a spreading delta system. The delta has fanned out into the Adriatic Sea to such an extent that today a number of cities are located on it, among them Adria.

What continent has almost no rivers?

Australia. Too large to be called an island, Australia is a continent set apart from Southeast Asia by enough distance and different kind of terrain to make it another world. The northern coastal strip is tropical and humid, and certain other coastal regions benefit from moist winds and the sea. Most of Australia, however, is a vast, dry bowl. Mountains cut off the interior and dry winds cannot provide generous rainfalls and resulting river systems. Many of the "rivers" that do exist are dry part of the year. The only dependable river system on the continent is the Murray in the southeast area.

The Golden Age of this city occurred five hundred years before the time of Christ.

What prominent city, once an ancient capital, nearly faded from existence?

It was a narrow escape for Athens, Greece. In the fourth and fifth centuries B.C., its "Golden Age," Athens was the largest and most glorious city of a culture that became the base for Western civilization. Then, because of wars, conquests, and neglect through the following centuries, Athens was allowed to decline. People who lived after the Golden Age did not appreciate the grand buildings that Greek artists, engineers, and architects had built. It was common practice, for example, to use marble fallen from magnificent buildings to make lime or building blocks. The classic Parthenon of the Acropolis, high above the city, was used as a powder magazine during a war with Turkey in 1645, and this masterpiece was almost destroyed in an explosion.

For many centuries, Greece was ruled by foreign powers, and by the early 1800's Athens had become a village of only 2,000 inhabitants. Fortunately, Greece won its independence in 1832, and Athens again began to grow. Today it is once more the largest Greek city (650,000 population). Modern Greeks appreciate the genius and skills of their ancient heritage, and they are working hard to build again upon their priceless background.

Where in the ancient world were ships carried overland?

Greece pushes out into the Mediterranean Sea like a gigantic inkblot, with a main peninsula, and many islands, inlets, bays, and capes. One large chunk of it, the Peloponnesus, just manages to be a part of the mainland by virtue of a slim connection between the Gulf of Corinth and the Saronic Gulf. About five miles of rocky land separate the two bodies of water.

In ancient times this neck of land presented great problems. For men engaged in trade or war, the isthmus was a tremendous inconvenience, and to avoid the long voyage around the Peloponnesus fair-sized ships were carted overland. Attempts to cut a canal through the land were frustrated because Greece is here, as elsewhere, rugged in terrain. The solution to the problem was not simply one of pushing a little dirt aside to make a channel.

The Romans worked on the idea. Caesar planned the cutting of a canal. In 67 A.D., Nero, while Emperor and on a concert tour of Greece, actually ordered the work started. Some progress was made, but the canal was not completed. Today there is a canal, made possible by modern machinery. It is a cut that jabs straight across the isthmus from gulf to gulf, through the rugged land. The precipitous sides of the channel hem in the ships as they take this short cut.

Two views of the Corinth Canal.

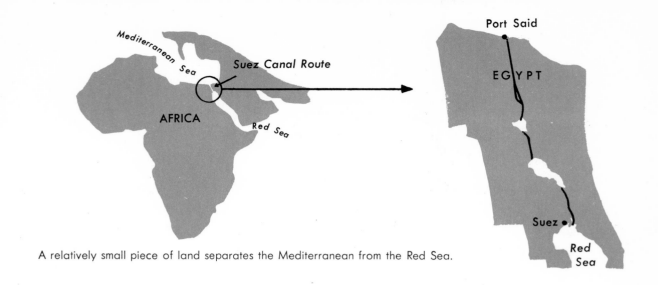

A relatively small piece of land separates the Mediterranean from the Red Sea.

Was the construction of the Suez Canal a modern idea?

Records show that as far back as 1800 B.C., Egyptians of the Feudal Age had built a canal from the northern end of the Red Sea to the nearest branch of the Nile in the eastern delta. Even in the ancient world man was aware that only a little land, comparatively speaking, separated the Mediterranean Sea from the Red Sea. With this knowledge also came the realization that being able to sail from one to the other would open a sea route that would be of great aid to commerce. Before long this first canal fell into disuse, for man had not yet learned how to build a permanent channel.

Rameses II, the great Pharaoh of Egypt who is believed to have been the ruler about the time of the Exodus, had a new canal built. After his death in 1234 B.C., the sands of the desert filled it up again.

Darius the Great, a Persian general, had the canal connecting the Mediterranean Sea and the Red Sea cut through again in 520 B.C. Other rulers worked on the canal until the eighth century A.D., when it was finally closed.

In 1798 when Napoleon invaded Egypt, he ordered a survey made. But it was not until the middle of the nineteenth century that a Frenchman, Ferdinand de Lesseps, was able to combine modern methods of engineering and finance to build the great cut that permits huge vessels to pass between the continents of Asia and Africa.

What great nation was made
possible by tremendous annual floods?

For at least six thousand years, Egypt has existed because of floods. It has built an entire culture—its whole civilization and agriculture—on the life-giving waters of the Nile River. Each September, although the climate is hot, clear, and dry, the great river overflows its banks and floods the fields that spread away on either side.

Great quantities of rich silt are left behind by these flood waters when they recede. Throughout the ages, the Egyptian farmer has depended upon this renewal of his fields by the Nile. Irrigation channels, storage basins, and diversion canals have been used for centuries to stretch out the period when the flood waters may be used. Every ounce of water that can be trapped and diverted must be put to work, for without the Nile, Egypt would be a desert wasteland.

In 1902 a dam was built at Aswan to store water and make irrigation possible over a longer period of time than the natural flood of the river provided. But the dam became inadequate, and today a new dam, the Aswan High Dam, is being built with Russian help. This dam will back up and store much more water than the first dam could store, and will make possible the irrigation of additional acres of Egypt's land.

Why do some Egyptians want
to fill up a huge hole in their country?

Only thirty miles from the Mediterranean Sea in the Libyan Desert of western Egypt is the Qattara Depression, 200 miles long and 436 feet below the level of the sea. Virtually a desert wasteland now, its character may be changed completely if a current idea is carried out.

The plan is to run a pipeline from the Mediterranean to a hydro-electric station that would be built at the edge of the depression. Sea water, rushing from the pipeline, would run through electric-generator turbines down into the huge cavity. The constant flow of water would generate electrical power which would be used over the years for industrial and civic development in the cities to the north and east of the Qattara Depression.

Perhaps twenty years of water flow would be required to fill the depression. The rapid evaporation of water under desert conditions would reduce the amount of water actually filling the depression, and so the salt content of the water would constantly increase. By the time the depression was filled, there would be a lake of high salt concentration. The electrical-power days would then be over and the lake would be mined for its concentration of chemicals from the sea. The economy of Egypt would be further assisted.

While this particular project may never be realized, it is an example of countless fascinating possibilities that are in the future for the engineer and scientist.

The modernization of Egypt is expensive for archaeology students. The impounded waters of the finished Aswan High Dam will flood a valley where priceless artifacts now stand.

Could an Iowa farmer collect starfish in his back yard?

Scores of museums around the world have evidence to prove that this has been done. Le Grand, a small town in central Iowa, is the site of a rock quarry which has provided building materials for a century. In 1858, James Hall, a geologist from New York, discovered crinoid fossil fragments at this spot. The crinoid is a member of the echinoderm family which includes sea urchins, sea lilies, sand dollars, and starfish. For forty years geologists and paleontologists came to Le Grand to search for these three-hundred-million-year-old specimens of fossil crinoids.

About 1900 a particularly rich find came to light at Le Grand, and one young man in the area developed a keen interest in fossil hunting. Although B. H. Beane turned to farming for his livelihood, his continued interest in science made him a very competent fossil hunter.

His reputation was established in 1931 when a blast at the quarry revealed a collection of numerous and almost perfect specimens. The understanding quarry owner allowed Beane to go over with great care the pieces removed from the quarry. Many were so detailed and unblemished that they are considered rarities. Some of these finds are now in many universities of the United States. Others are in museums around the world. Beane's careful approach to the task of fossil finding rewarded him with world-wide attention.

Why should a fisherman be careful
tying up his boat in Passamaquoddy Bay, New Brunswick?

Passamaquoddy Bay is on the Bay of Fundy, the area of the greatest tides on earth. In some sections along the shore of this bay the tidal range is fifty feet!

Fishing-boat activity in waters such as these is strictly regulated to the hours when the water is safely high. At other times, boats not out in the Bay of Fundy or at sea will be resting on the mud of the inlets and bays along the shore. Every dock will sit high and dry at low tide, and any boat thoughtlessly tied up with a taut line at high tide will be "hanging on the ropes," or broken loose, by the drop in the water as the tide went out—and *down*.

The flow of water from these tides is so immense and so regular that for years men have thought of harnessing the natural forces. It is estimated that two billion tons of water are carried into Passamaquoddy Bay alone, twice each day—a hundred billion tons in the Bay of Fundy itself. If suitable dams, spillways, and locks could be developed and built, vast amounts of electric power could be generated by turbines turned by a controlled flow of these waters.

Low tide in Passamaquoddy Bay.

Does the surface of the earth move?

Of course we know that the earth spins on its axis and moves around the sun. We also know that the surface heaves and falls at a slow rate over great lengths of time. If the theories about the drifting of continents are valid, the surface itself moves to and fro through ages of time. But the surface also moves up and down constantly like a breathing giant.

The tidal—gravitational—pull of the sun and moon acts upon the land areas as on the seas, and the surface of the earth is known to pulsate through a twenty-four hour period with a rise of as much as six inches on the North American continent.

Earthquakes are responsible for another form of surface movement, sudden violent shifts up or down along a "fault" or parallel to it. The disastrous earthquake of 1923 in Japan was of the first sort. It caused the floor of Tokyo Bay to fall, drawing half the water level out of connecting canals and rivers of Yokohama in minutes. The great Alaska earthquake of 1964 combined both types of movement.

Where is Cuba in relation to the United States?

Cincinnati, Ohio, is almost directly north of the western tip of Cuba. Almost half of the island lies west of the Atlantic coast side of Florida. Havana, the Cuban capital, in the western portion of the island, is almost directly south of St. Petersburg, which is on the Gulf, or west, coast of Florida. Key West, the southernmost point of the United States, is less than a hundred miles from Havana in a northeast by north direction. With Fidel Castro in power in Cuba, troubled relations between that country and the United States have made Cuba a barrier for commercial air traffic flying south from Florida. A special air corridor over Cuba had to be arranged to fly directly from Florida to Jamaica.

What country, located on the Pacific Ocean, has a port which docks ships coming directly from the Atlantic?

In South America, for almost two thousand miles in a straight-line measurement, the Amazon River and its tributaries drain the tropical rainforest belt running east from the Andes Mountains to the Atlantic Ocean. Boats using this waterway can travel almost all the way across the continent at its widest point.

The Andes Mountains are a coastal range running through Peru. On the eastern side of these mountains, on the Amazon River, is the Peruvian city of Iquitos. It is a port city for ships coming up the Amazon from the Atlantic Ocean.

What states of the U.S.A. are closer to Asia than to Washington, D.C.?

An idea of how international a nation the United States is can be gained by a little study of a globe. Alaska and Hawaii are obviously close to Asia. The Bering Strait separates Alaska from Russia by only about 50 miles. Is this area, U.S. islands are within sight of Russian islands; there is only 2.5 miles between Big Diomede Island (Russian) and Little Diomede Island (U.S.). Hawaii stretches about 1,650 miles toward the mainland of Asia, across the vastness of the Pacific; Honolulu is 1,000 miles closer to Tokyo, Japan, than to Washington, D.C.

Other states are closer to Asia than one might first think. Much of the state of Washington is closer to Asia than to the United States' capital. Oregon is halfway between our capital and Asia; the northern coast of California is closer to Asia. The U.S.A. couldn't be isolated if it wanted to. Nome, Alaska, is about the same distance from Washington, D.C., as it is from Shanghai, China.

Modern-day Mexico City.

What national capital is built on a former lake?

When the Spanish conquerors under Cortés came to this continent in 1519, they found a fabulous Aztec city, Tenochtitlan, built on an island in the midst of the waters of Lake Texcoco. This city was the forerunner of modern Mexico City. The city had been founded in 1325, and the Aztecs had developed a metropolis of beautiful temples, large markets, and magnificent floating gardens. It was connected by bridges to the mainland. In the siege of 1521 the ancient city was all but destroyed by the Spanish, who then rebuilt it on its site. Eventually Lake Texcoco became so shallow it set forth obnoxious odors and had to be drained. Mexico City expanded onto land that was the former lake bed, and even today the residents are faced with the problem of their buildings sinking into the soft marshy ground.

Has anyone ever seen a volcano forming?

In 1943, a sheepherder named Dionisio Pulido was tending his flock in his field 125 miles due west of Mexico City. At about noon Pulido noticed smoke coming out of the ground in thin, white columns. By four o'clock in the afternoon flames, dense smoke, explosions and loud noises were observed. In five days Pulido had a volcanic cone 300 feet high in his field, explosively active at the rate of seventeen blasts a minute. In ten days there was a 722-foot mountain in the field. By its first full year of activity, this volcanic peak, now named Paricutín, was a magnificent 1,410 feet above the pasture!

Paricutín is in an area of known volcanic activity. There had been earthquakes immediately beforehand to warn of something coming. Despite the great age of most of the prominent features of the world's landscape, there are some rather large bits of scenery that are not only new, but have formed before our eyes.

Could volcanic activity
inside the earth cause it to blow up?

Volcanic explosions, as we know them, are concentrated blow-ups in one area. Because the crust of the earth is not strong and even enough for forces inside the planet to build up destructive pressure everywhere, a massive explosion cannot occur. The "safety-valves" of local volcanic eruptions prevent this happening.

Do islands ever disappear?

They can and do, but not very often. In 1831 a volcano appeared in the Mediterranean Sea, forming a new island which became known as Graham's Island. Because it was made up of loose volcanic material, it was soon broken up by wave action, and it became a shoal, a shallow place in the sea.

In some cases, islands have risen from the sea in violent volcanic eruptions, boiling the sea water, sending clouds of steam and smoke high into the air, and have then collapsed into the sea again. Not all of the surface features of earth are here long enough to be worn down by the long-term forces of nature!

Do all volcanoes smoke?

No, not always, and unless you're very smart about volcanoes, don't build a house on one just because it doesn't smoke.

Many volcanoes are considered dormant (sleeping soundly and not expected to awaken soon), or extinct (dead and cold). Although much of the ground we live on is volcanic in origin, in most cases the activity happened so long ago that evidence is quite well hidden. Any volcanoes in the area are extinct, and volcanic activity is regarded as long since ended. The countryside of France is like this. There are castles atop volcanic cores that are quite dead.

A dormant volcano is another story. Photographs of the crater of Irazu in Costa Rica, taken only a few years ago, showed roads leading up to its edge and quiet brooding pools down in its silent and closed mouth. In the spring of 1963 it became a violently erupting beast. Ashes and smoke threatened the very existence of San Jose and other spots nearby. Tons of ashes are swept off the streets daily, and the people find breathing difficult as the volcano fills the air with expelled material.

Where in the world did an island blow up in the greatest explosion known to modern man?

On August 27, 1883, a small island in the Sunda Strait, between Sumatra and Java, in what is now known as Indonesia, literally blew its top. An active volcano in a part of the world renowned for them, Krakatoa exploded with such force that rocks from its interior were hurled 34 miles. The sound was heard 3,000 miles away and was thought to be the roar of heavy guns. Walls in a town 100 miles distant were cracked, and tidal waves were started that took 36,000 lives on nearby islands. Dust settled for 10 days afterward as far away as 3,000 miles. Fine dust that did not fall in the period immediately after the catastrophe spread over the skies of the world, and brilliant red sunsets were common, world-wide, well into the next year.

Geologists think that a huge chamber under the volcano was emptied in the explosion, bringing on an inward collapse and swallowing the mountain top.

Krakatoa has a child today, Anak, on the same site, born in 1930. Alone in the strait now, it may grow to violence some day too.

The fine dust from this explosion spread to the skies of the world.

Did the moon come out of the Pacific Ocean?

This is one of those fascinating theories that may be given additional support, or disproved, by man's exploration of the moon some day soon.

In 1879 George H. Darwin, son of the famous Charles Darwin, suggested that the earth, originally molten and spinning rapidly, developed bulges from the spinning. He believed it possible that at a particular moment when the pull of the sun and the centrifugal force of the spinning earth were greatest, a massive blob of molten material spun off the earth, coursed into space, and cooled to a spherical shape as the moon, our natural satellite. The most likely place on earth from which the material came was thought to be the Pacific Ocean.

Other theories, including that of the drifting apart of the continents from a supercontinent, have been tied into the Pacific idea. Some said that the drift of the continents was in compensation for the uneven surface after the spinning off of the moon material.

Not so, said scientists of more recent years. During the 1930's Darwin's theory was discredited. Many reasons were advanced against it. For one thing, it was said that the mass of material destined to be the moon could not have survived the forces and journey into space intact. It would have broken into bits. Another pointed out that there is not sufficient proof that the floor of the Pacific is different in basic structure from the Atlantic, that the two ocean bottoms would have to be fundamentally different if such a cataclysm occurred.

Recently, despite continued skepticism on the part of many scientists, the theory has been revived. The uneven consistency in the molten earth is said to have unbalanced it, and the unstable mass threw off the moon. Those proposing the revived theory have refined certain aspects of it. If proven true, our moon can then be regarded as not only a close companion but a blood relative. That the earth was once molten and that the Pacific floor is different from the Atlantic floor are two fundamentals that would be of great importance to man's knowledge.

The Aurora Borealis of northern skies.

What causes the Northern Lights?

The Aurora Borealis, or Northern Lights, are evidence of the discharge of particles of energy from the sun (93,000,000 miles distant). The magnetic field of the earth extends out into space in a doughnut-shaped volume with the hole of the doughnut located at the magnetic north and south polar regions. This field traps solar energy, and under certain conditions, at altitudes of from fifty to six hundred miles, visible light will be emitted by the energy.

How far south have the Northern Lights been seen?

The Northern Lights have been observed about as far south as New Orleans, Louisiana. At latitudes of about 70 degrees N. Magnetic, these auroras can be seen about two nights out of three. The area with the maximum of activity is on a line running roughly from Hudson Bay to Point Barrow, Alaska.

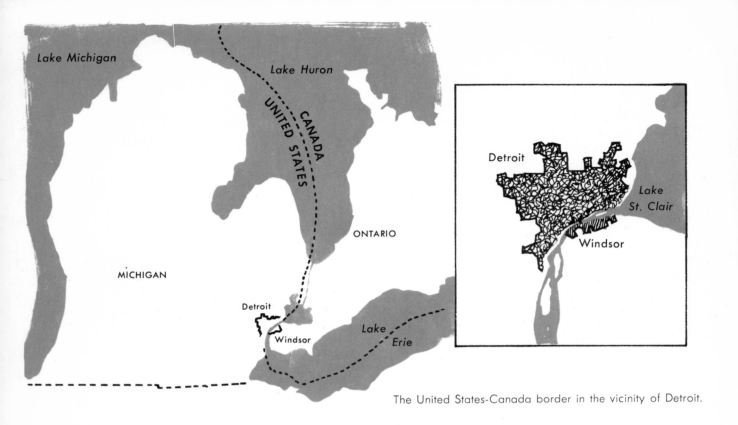

The United States-Canada border in the vicinity of Detroit.

In which direction would you go from Detroit to reach the closest Canadian point?

You could go either across the Ambassador Bridge or through the tunnel under the Detroit River into Windsor. In so doing, you would go almost due south! Lake St. Clair, east of Detroit, drains westward into the Detroit River. South of this is a southwestern tip of the Province of Ontario, Canada.

Directly related to this geographical "believe it or not," and to the friendly relations between Canada and the United States, is the interesting fact that many trains operating from the seaboard area between New York and Maine travel to Detroit, Michigan, through Canada. They follow a route through Ontario to avoid a longer trip entirely through United States territory. The shortcut from Buffalo, New York, to Windsor, Canada, and across the bridge into Detroit is made with little attention to the fact that national borders are being crossed.

Why do people build dams?

Dams are multipurpose tools. They bring a river under control by spreading out its rate of flow over an extended period of time. Dams create reservoirs in which the excess flow of a river can gather month after month. The flow of water from this reservoir is then regulated by spillways and overflow to maintain a steady stream of water below the dam. The accumulated water can be used to provide power by causing it to flow through turbine blades connected to generators for the manufacture of electricity; or it can be used as an inland lake for water sports.

In these basic ways, dams can provide a solution to flooding problems in an area, keep the river flow steady and always under control, and harness the mass of water to do useful work for man.

Do dams interfere with river traffic?

While there are cases where dams are a nuisance to boat traffic on rivers, the opposite is true so much of the time that it is startling.

Dams are often the thing which makes a river navigable. Without controlled river flow and the building of river depth upstream from dams, many rivers are not consistently deep enough to navigate. True, a dam will require that boats go through locks to go past the site up or down the river. However, this is a small hindrance compared to river channels of uncertain depth and widely varying rate of flow.

What famous city, founded because of a salt monopoly, has no streets and is sinking into the sea?

Venice, Italy, was built on islands formed by silt deposits. Long before Columbus discovered the New World, Venice grew wealthy and powerful from a natural supply of a valuable common necessity, salt. For about three hundred years it had been an important city, jealously guarding the political power which salt gave to it. The city's master builders were men of imagination who employed the best artisans, artists, and architects of the Middle Ages. We can thank them today for an unusual and beautiful city with canals, instead of streets, which are crossed by arched bridges and lined with palaces and fine homes.

Unfortunately for everyone, this unique city is not built on a solid rock foundation. The silt deposits continue to build the land, giving the city serious problems: how to maintain the canals at an adequate depth and how to keep the buildings from sinking into the soft ground on which they are built.

144

What scar on the surface of the earth was made by an object from outer space?

Near Winslow, Arizona, about a hundred miles southeast of the Grand Canyon is Meteor Crater, which measures 4,000 feet across and 600 feet deep. With its edge rising about 150 feet above the surrounding plain, this is one of the best places on earth to imagine yourself in a moon crater. The deep-dish shape of the crater produces shadow patterns in the morning and afternoon that remind one of the appearance of a lunar landscape as seen through powerful binoculars or telescopes. Meteor Crater is so eroded from weathering that it is probably quite different in surface texture from the moon, but the basic similarity is fascinating.

The ridge surrounding the crater is made up of immense blocks of rock. There are rock fragments six miles from the site, apparently thrown there by a gigantic explosion. Many tons of iron meteorites have been found in the immediate area, and testing by scientists has proved that the pit was made by an immense meteor from outer space. The meteor mass, weighing thousands of tons and traveling at, perhaps 36,000 miles per hour, is believed to have created this spectacular crater some fifty thousand years ago.

Where is the world's highest active volcano?

Ecuador, South America, possesses the highest, actively smoking mountain on earth. This mountain, Cotopaxi, is 19,344 feet high, and is part of the Andes range of mountains. As a matter of fact, the entire Andes range has been built by direct volcanic action, and the highest volcanic mountain on earth, Aconcagua, 22,834 feet high, is in the Andes range. Located in the country of Argentina, it is an inactive volcano.

What happens to the millions of gallons of water that spill out of a huge Russian lake and seem to disappear?

The Caspian Sea, the world's largest salt lake, receives waters from the Volga and Ural rivers, as well as several other minor ones. The Caspian is about 3,000 feet deep in places, and its surface is usually 92 feet below sea level. The level of the Caspian is not constant, however; over the years it varies as the amount of water brought by the rivers varies.

During the last part of the nineteenth century, the rivers brought so much water that the Caspian overflowed its banks. A natural dike which separated it from a depression immediately to the east, in the Kara Kum Desert, broke. The depression filled with Caspian waters, and the break in the dike remained, developing into a permanent passage between the two bodies of water, known now as the Proliv Karabogaskiy.

The level of the Caspian eventually fell again, but the passage or strait remained. Each year it drains two cubic miles of water from the Caspian into the desert depression or gulf, called the Kara-Bogaz-Gol. This is the huge hole in the ground into which the water seems to disappear, and many local stories have developed about the hole and the disappearing water. The gulf, once 42 feet deep, is now only 10 feet deep.

The real reason for the drop in the level of the gulf waters is *evaporation*. The dry, burning east wind of the desert pulls moisture out of the gulf and turns its waters into the saltiest of all bodies of water on earth. They are so salty that a profitable salt recovery industry mines the precious chemical deposits for industrial use.

What city, built to order, cost thousands of lives in the making and has had three names?

Peter the Great was faced with a problem which faces the Russians even today—the problem of adequate all-year, all-weather ports. In spite of its great size, its location in both Europe and Asia, and its great natural resources, the U.S.S.R. is locked in by geography. At the European end of the country, Russia does not have the warm-water, convenient ports of other European nations. Far to the east, the U.S.S.R is bounded by the Pacific, but the tremendous distance from the industrial heart of European Russia to the east coast makes trading and shipping through Pacific ports impractical.

Hoping to solve this continuing problem, Czar Peter in 1703 ordered a city built on the Gulf of Finland on some land he had just won from Sweden. The marshland location and the poor climate made construction very difficult, and thousands of lives were lost in the building. Nevertheless, St. Petersburg was completed, and it became the capital city of the czars and Russia's "window to the west." Later it was renamed Petrograd, "Peter City." Then, following the Bolshevik Revolution in 1917, Petrograd became Leningrad, and the capital was moved back to Moscow.

The "Window to the West."

Where in the world is there a country composed of thousands of islands?

There are two countries that fit this description. One is the Philippines, which consists of about seven thousand islands. Thirteen out of every fourteen of these are less than one square mile in area, and many of them do not even have a name. The other country is the relatively new Republic of Indonesia, which consists of innumerable islands stretching over three thousand miles from one end of the group to the other.

Is it true that North and South America were once joined to Europe and Africa?

Looking at a globe or map of the world, it is easy to become intrigued by the curious coincidence in the coasts on each side of the Atlantic. The shore lines of North and South America look as if they would fit, like a jigsaw-puzzle, into the shore lines of Europe and Africa. This is especially true south of the equator—South America and Africa appear to have simply drifted apart. Aside from minor variations that erosion could explain, they appear matched. So strong is the suggestion of fit that many scientists have been lead to undertake extensive study of evidence that might explain the coincidence.

One theory, discarded for some years until it recently regained attention, is that of "continental drift." In this it is stated that the land masses of the earth are floating on a thick, sticky mantle underneath that allows movement to occur over great periods of time. "Floating on" in this case refers to no liquid common to our everyday experience. The mantle under the rock crust of the earth would have currents that move perhaps an inch a year in some places. This slight movement over a period of two hundred million years could have broken up one vast super-continent covering much of one-half of the earth.

148

But this is merely a theory. Not enough is known about the interior of the earth to prove conclusively the drifting of the continents. It will be many more years before we can determine whether the Americas were once joined to Europe and Africa.

What continent has been described as a peninsula and as a bundle of peninsulas?

Europe is really a peninsula, a very large one. Between the waters off Scandinavia and the Mediterranean Sea it is a thrust of land out from the great land mass of Asia. This large peninsula is, in turn, made up of the Scandinavian peninsula (Norway and Sweden), the peninsula of Finland, then Denmark. France is peninsular, and the Iberian peninsula of Portugal and Spain adjoins it. The Italian peninsula juts into the Mediterranean Sea, and Greece lies at the tip of another peninsula to the east. Little of Europe is a great distance from deep-water shipping lanes, and this fact has helped keep Europe prosperous and active in world trade channels.

A peninsula made up of peninsulas.

Why were the Tigris and Euphrates rivers so important in ancient history?

From the Persian Gulf to the Mediterranean Sea lies an area where the normal rainfall is so scant that, if it weren't for rivers that originate in mountains to the north, the land would be quite parched. Two of these rivers come down from the rugged terrain of Turkey and join together shortly before dumping into the Persian Gulf. They are the Tigris and Euphrates rivers, and they were the life blood of what may have been the beginnings of civilization.

In the earliest days the area had enough grassland, nourished by a small amount of rainfall in the winter, to support wandering nomads. Some of these nomads grouped together in settlements, a few of which developed into major centers. Here, it is thought, was the Garden of Eden, the Biblical site of man's origin.

The two rivers were tapped by extensive irrigation systems that caused the wasteland to blossom. Babylon, south of today's Baghdad, developed as a treasure city whose splendor came from a culture developed along the Euphrates two thousand years before Christ. This civilization was given force by a people called Sumerians. The Babylonians smelted metals and carried on extensive commerce. They had a form of writing, irrigated agriculture, the wheel, and domesticated animals. Along with the Egyptians, who lived practically next door, the Babylonians seem to have started mankind on its road to development.

Could the splendid Hanging Gardens of Babylon have looked like this?

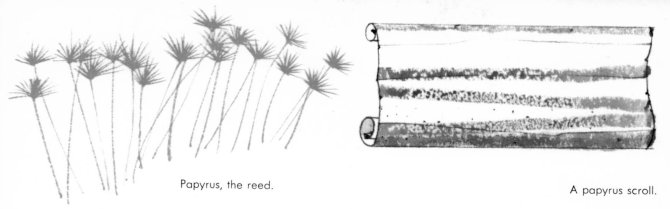

Papyrus, the reed.

A papyrus scroll.

How did a simple plant growing in Egypt help change the world?

At least two thousand years before Christ, the Egyptians discovered that the river reed *papyrus* could be split into thin strips, flattened, and pasted in layers to form a writing surface. By overlapping the edges of papyrus sheets, they learned further to form writing surfaces of almost any desired width and length. From the Greek word *papyr* (*papyros* with the Greek grammatical ending) we have obtained our word paper.

Using for ink water thickened with vegetable gum and darkened with soot, and with a pointed reed as a pen, the Egyptians wrote on papyrus with a system of symbols that began as pictures of the object or the subject referred to. This system developed into a phonetic system in which the picture would indicate a sound that referred to ideas. With this system, the Egyptians gave to western civilization a method of recording information far more suitable than the cumbersome clay tablet of other peoples, and developed a system of symbols, an "alphabet," that made it possible to pass along involved ideas without the need to talk to people face to face.

Once man was free to conveniently record ideas, stories, plans, and information, he was then on the road to making the most of one of his many unique advantages over other animals. Because he had a means of accumulating, gathering, and distributing knowledge, he could learn from others whom he never saw. A chimpanzee may be alert and sharp of sense and dextrous, but he knows no more than a chimpanzee of five thousand years ago, because there is no chimpanzee store of knowledge passed on to him.

151

Where in the United States
is there a rain forest?

The term "rain forest" usually is applied to such tropical areas as the Amazon region of South America. But the term is especially applicable to a forest in the state of Washington. The Olympic Peninsula, which is at the extreme northwest tip of conterminous United States, is subject to fog and rain caused by the moisture-laden air coming in from the Pacific Ocean. Almost 150 inches of rain fall here each year. A steady succession of weather "fronts" promotes woodland growth that is so thick the shafts of sunlight in clearing weather reach the ground only occasionally.

Western red cedar and western hemlock trees tower two hundred feet above a forest floor covered with moss and vines. Douglas fir trees grow to great heights where clearings allow sunlight to penetrate. Saplings take root on the fallen branches and trunks of dead trees. The names of the trees in the Olympic forest are not those of the vegetation in a tropical rain forest, but the appearance of the forest, nevertheless, reminds you of an equatorial jungle.

Where is there a lake called
"You fish on your side, we fish on our side,
nobody fish in middle"?

Lake Chaubunagungamaug is the shortened version of a 44-lettered name, translated from the Algonquin Indian language. It is near Webster, Massachusetts, and is also known as Webster Lake. One can imagine the council of peace that agreed upon the conditions stated in its unusual name. Do you suppose the Indians met in the middle of the lake and passed a peace pipe from canoe to canoe?

Fog can be beautiful and treacherous.

Where is there the most fog?

Meteorologists say there is a fog when visibility is less than 1,100 yards. The foggiest area on earth is considered to be the Grand Banks of Newfoundland. Here the chill Labrador Current flows southward from the Arctic and meets the comparatively warm Gulf Stream with its equatorial and Caribbean waters. The result is frequent fogs.

Before the development of radar, the North Atlantic fog was a deadly hazard to navigation. Captains traveling through this area frequently were forced to slow their ships to a snail's pace, all the time sounding their foghorns, or to bring them to a complete halt until the fog lifted. The Grand Banks fog, coupled with the possible presence of icebergs drifting down the Labrador Current, was a combination which made night travel across the North Atlantic very dangerous.

Are there any insects in the Antarctic?

In spite of the uninviting climate of the South Polar regions, there is land-type life there. Scientists who have explored the few square miles of ice-free rocks in the Antarctic have found tiny wingless flies and spring-tails. In addition, at least one member of the spider family, the tiny mite, has been identified. Many forms of life exist in the salt waters around the continent, but there is little insect life as we know it on the land.

Where in the world does it rain without getting the ground wet?

Conditions of extreme heat and dry air over such deserts as those of the United States' Southwest help to keep the deserts as they are. Desert rain clouds are scarce enough normally, of course, and often rain that does manage to fall over the desert doesn't do any good. Clouds can be seen releasing precious water in generous showers without a drop reaching the parched soil. The extremely dry, hot air near the surface of the earth will evaporate the raindrops, turning them back into vapor before they can touch the ground. Like magic, the falling rain disappears.

Where can you catch shrimp in the desert?

There are several places, oddly enough. You have to know where and when to look.

In 1955 an eighteen-inch downpour flooded Bicycle Dry Lake in the Mojave Desert. It was the first significant rainfall this desert basin had

had in twenty-five years. Within two days, millions of tiny fresh-water shrimp were swarming in the water. On land about as dry as land can be, a store of shrimp eggs had been waiting for a quarter of a century to be brought to life by the presence of water.

There was nation-wide publicity about this when it happened—but it is actually something which is an annual event in certain deserts when there is enough rain. Shrimp eggs stay in the hardened floors of the Sonora and Chihuahua deserts until the rains come each summer. The sun-heated water rapidly incubates the eggs. Several varieties of shrimp come to life, live a short while, and lay eggs to be hatched the following year.

Scientists believe that perhaps a million years ago the ancestors of these shrimp gradually adjusted to a change from life in "permanent" waters in these regions to a life dependent upon uncertain water supplies. As the water supply gradually diminished, the surviving shrimp eggs found it necessary to adapt to a long wait, as much as a hundred years, locked in the hardened mud bottoms, for moisture in which to hatch.

Does a ship weigh more or less in the moonlight?

Gravity is a phenomenon that acts with the speed of light. The position of the moon in the sky almost instantly affects our ocean tides and the surface of the earth. Similarly, the position of the moon in the sky also affects other objects on earth. An ocean liner cruising the open sea with the moon nearly overhead will push down into the water with less force than when the moon is on the horizon, because some of the ship's weight is being attracted by the moon's gravity. Therefore a ship weighs less in the moonlight, and least when the moon is directly overhead.

Why do scientists plan to go out to sea to drill a hole through the crust of the earth?

The crust of the earth is composed basically of sedimentary, granite, and basalt rocks ranging in thickness from about twenty miles to four miles. It is known to be thickest under the continents and thinnest under the sea. The crust's depth is similar to the thickness of the base of a floating iceberg. The berg that towers high above the water line has a base that goes down deep in the sea, while a small berg has a relatively shallower base. The height of the continents above the bottom of the sea is accompanied by similarly greater depth of the crust.

The crust is thought to be a material which floats over a deep rock mantle, and the line of separation between the crust and the mantle is called the Mohorovicic discontinuity. Scientists are now working on a project to drill down through this discontinuity into the mantle. The project is called Mohole, after the name of the line of separation. Scientists believe that direct knowledge of the mantle material will help them understand what the surface of the earth was like when it was first formed. Since its formation, the mantle has been covered with sedimentary rocks, volcanic flows, seas, and countless foldings and fracturings of this covering.

Logically, a drilling operation to get to the mantle should be in areas where the mantle is closest, where the crust is thinnest. So the Mohole will be dug at sea, even though there may be one-half mile of sediment and a few miles of crust under two and one half miles of water in the locations being explored at this time.

The Mohole will be a tremendous job. Test drilling in shallow waters, using a special barge as the drilling platform, has already shown that the idea may be sound. It will be difficult in many respects, including the bringing up of core samples from the drilling. But if it is successful, the project will allow man to see and analyze the basic building material of the earth.

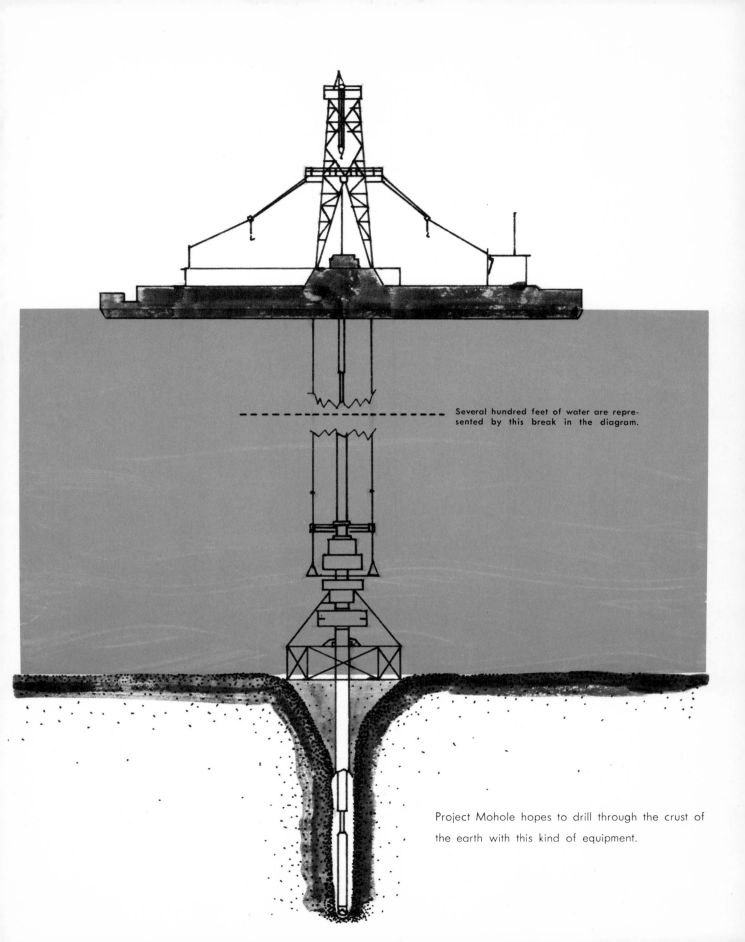

Several hundred feet of water are represented by this break in the diagram.

Project Mohole hopes to drill through the crust of the earth with this kind of equipment.

Is the Gulf of California surrounded by
the shores of United States or Mexico?

The Gulf of California is a body of water separating almost all of the narrow Baja California Peninsula from the major part of Mexico. A small difference in land or sea level would cut off the peninsula from Mexico, and it would be joined then only to the state of California, which borders it immediately to the north.

Through the portion of the peninsula at the head of the gulf—about forty to sixty miles wide between the United States border and the gulf —the Colorado River makes its way to the sea, laden with silt. As the waters empty into the Gulf of California, the silt is deposited at the mouth, building up the land. Each year the silt deposits make the gulf a tiny bit smaller.

Where are there people whose bodies
have changed because of their environment?

Bolivia is located just inland from the Pacific Coast and about midway between the northern and southern tips of South America. It is populated mainly by Indians, with few persons of pure European stock. Bolivia as a nation suffers because its resources and agriculture have not been sufficiently developed. It does have some mineral resources; tin is the one most extensively mined today.

The high plateau country where most of the people live is about 12,000 feet above sea level. The Andes Mountains rise another 10,000 feet above these highlands. Bolivia's tin mines are in the mountains, at altitudes far above the 12,000-foot plateau.

Over a period of many years of living and working at these altitudes, the Bolivian Indians have become a people with greater lung capacity than those of us who live where the air is not so thin. Also, they tend to be shorter, and they have a circulatory system which is very well suited to living where air pressure is less than it is at lower altitudes. Generation after generation, these Indians gradually developed into humans physically different from the men who live and work at lower altitudes and greater air pressure.

Which is longer, a nautical mile or a statute mile?

The nautical mile is longer. The statute mile contains 5,280 feet, and today the nautical mile equals 6,076.115 feet, or 1,852 meters.

The nautical mile is related directly to the degrees into which the surface of the earth has been divided. One nautical mile is the length of 1/60th of one degree of latitude; 1/60th of a degree is called a minute. This is no simple matter, however, for the earth is not perfectly spherical.

Britain set the nautical mile at 6,080 feet, and for a while the United States used a 6,080.20-foot figure, the length of one minute on a perfect sphere whose area is equal to the area of the earth. In July, 1959, official United States' recognition was given to the 6,076.115-foot international nautical mile.

What other questions do you have about the world?

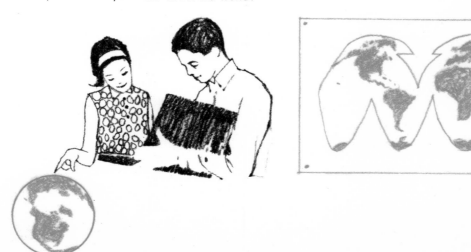

INDEX

PRINTED IN U.S.A.